Six and a Half Years on a Dunghill

Life in Specialist Disability Accommodation

by

Peter Gibilisco

Foreword by

Bruce C. Wearne

CCB Publishing
British Columbia, Canada

Six and a Half Years on a Dunghill:
Life in Specialist Disability Accommodation

ISBN-13 978-1-77143-376-1
First Edition

Library and Archives Canada Cataloguing in Publication
Title: Six and a half years on a dunghill : life in specialist disability accommodation / by Peter Gibilisco ; foreword by Bruce C. Wearne.
Names: Gibilisco, Peter, 1962- author.
Description: Includes bibliographical references.
Identifiers: Canadiana (print) 20190052562 | Canadiana (ebook) 20190052600 | ISBN 9781771433761 (softcover) | ISBN 9781771433778 (PDF)
Subjects: LCSH: People with disabilities—Services for. | LCSH: People with disabilities—Social conditions. | LCSH: People with disabilities—Economic conditions. | LCSH: People with disabilities—Government policy. | LCSH: Human rights. | LCSH: Social justice.
Classification: LCC HV1568 .G53 2019 | DDC 362.4—dc23

Cover artwork: Photo of Peter Gibilisco courtesy of Michael Silver

Publisher: CCB Publishing
British Columbia, Canada
www.ccbpublishing.com

Contents

PREFACE

This 6 ½ years (July 2011 – February 2018) in shared supported accommodation, has had a significant impact on the deterioration of my disability. This attains to using the phrase 'on a dunghill' as a description of my life in a shared supported facility. This term of expression gives readers an idea of the ugly reality; of the helplessness, immobility, failure to speak and see; and of course the power of irritation towards the delivery of life circumstances pertaining to the disability sector. This bureaucratic mess is subsequent to a lack of true empathy, which may conflict with any budget bottom line, thus enforcing the creation of social dilemmas which then draws attention away from the original problem. This is something that can also be performed by non-government authorities, as is seen in my own circumstance.

This book, therefore, is to focus truthfully on many self-explosive happenings in my life in shared support accommodation. The constraints that I felt personally through a gradual but detrimental loss of control has left me with a form of mental torture.

I therefore need to get out, because of my undue treatment.

ACKNOWLEDGEMENTS

I wish to dedicate this book to the most intelligent, inspiring and warm-hearted friend and colleague, BRUCE WEARNE; he has helped me in life and to achieve academic excellence.

Secondly, my academic support worker, CHRISTINA IRUGALBANDARA, a beautiful young lady and brilliant academic.

Also my excellent and caring professional editor, SUSAN PRIOR.

Thank you to my past PhD supervisor, TIM MARJORIBANKS.

Frank Stilwell, an excellent and a good friend.

Paul Rabinovitch, whose support work can be witnessed in this text.

Pat Stretton, the wife of my important and deceased colleague who I continually think about.

And all who helped with the reviews.

FOREWORD: Pushing on for Justice

This book brings together in one document, the reflections of a remarkable fellow who keeps on pushing for justice. This is a task that has preoccupied Peter Gibilisco in all his waking moments for decades. In the pages that follow, Peter tells his own story while issuing a call for greater awareness of the complex task that awaits us to ensure safe and just structures and processes of care for those whose abilities to contribute are severely constrained by bodily malfunction, disease or injury.

Not everyone can publish material that openly draws attention to his or her own 'bag of bones', let alone one of bodily constraints that bring with them personal and intimate disappointments arising from such 'disability'. These are deeply personal issues and those who do make their contribution publicly and in publications have learned to do so without worrying too much about the image projected when 'talking' with the help of a computer robotic voice or describing one's situation on the page, or computer screen.

There is something inspiring here and I would invite readers to think deeply about this problematic as they consider Peter's persistent push for justice for the severely disabled. Here in this publication Peter is giving voice to his 'beef' about the ideology that propels the management of supported accommodation.

As much as this book is advice to social policy researchers and managers of 'disability services' - published strategically at a time when NDIS is being rolled out - it is also autobiographical, drawing upon his own experiences. His contribution assumes that much more is at stake than merely ensuring his own sense of satisfaction at having given voice to his critique and suggestions for reform.

I have known Peter for over 20 years, since he first knocked on my door at the Frankston Campus of Monash University. He struggled up the poorly disability-equipped elevator in his wheelchair to my second floor office. He asked to be included in the "Introduction to Sociology" Summer Semester course I was teaching. One thing led to another and, as he tells it, he became an enthusiastic student who eventually concentrated on sociology and even developed the outrageous long-term aim of bringing the disciplines of sociology and economics together in some kind of creative symbiosis. These days he would say that sociology and economics need to overcome a loss of "synergy". That was the start of our friendship.

First our friendship grew from a relationship of lecturer and student; then I became his Honours supervisor and when he pushed on further up the higher education mountain-range, I became his MA dissertation supervisor as he chose to write a Masters Thesis on Hugh Stretton, the critical historical economist who had done much to bring economics and sociology together. During this time I departed from the University.

Since then, Peter went on to gain a PhD and a reputation among prominent economists for his brazen jet-setting willingness to knock on academic doors around the country as part of his refusal to allow his condition to prevent his mobile mind from pushing ahead with what had to be done. In more recent decades, I have acted as his proof-reader as we have looked carefully at social policy, as fellow members of this Australian political community doing what we can to promote public justice.

In March 2006 he graduated with a doctorate from Melbourne University, and from then on became a regular contributor to Graham Young's On Line Opinion.

Recent years have not been all plain sailing for Peter. And what we have here are the ongoing reflections of a social justice activist. Peter works. His body may be inert and incapable of what we might say are 'normal' physiological responses, but the arrival of this publication is evidence of his persistent effort to "push back" against the frustration that such restrictions bring with them. Readers, like myself, can have little knowledge of how frustrating a day-by-day experience under these conditions can be. So I counsel readers that when what you read seems tinged with bitterness keep in mind that Peter is "pushing back" against being overwhelmed by the debilitations of Friedreich's Ataxia. His aim is clearly to keep his own responsibility as an advocate for social justice on his and our horizon.

Well done, Peter. We're in your debt. Thanks for continuing to push on with the task of promoting social justice!

Bruce C. Wearne
Point Lonsdale
Sunday, 11 February 2018

AS I SEE IT: WRITING WITH BACK TO THE WALL

Memorandum: by Bruce C. Wearne

Let me try and explain to you how I see your wrestling with Peter's manuscript. I hope it might help you get further insight into the subtlety of what he is banging on about.

It is now a few months shy of 20 years ago since I, as Peter's MA thesis supervisor, walked out of a Monash University Arts Faculty meeting. I left because half-way through its proceedings the Dean announced that it had become a meeting of the academic industrial union. A miraculous transformation, but part of a serious erosion of university integrity.

That was the tipping point for me and I decided to apply for "Very Early Retirement". Peter's work was not complete at that point and the "retirement" was contracted with an agreement that I remain supervisor and help Peter bring his work to completion. This I was only too happy to do. Since then, Peter and I have kept in contact and he and I have continued to discuss his contribution to public policy and social justice for the severely disabled.

Peter subsequently gained a PhD from Melbourne University and I've been privileged to watch his "progress". Now that word "progress"; it is in inverted commas. As Peter knows only too well, and which we, his friends, colleagues and assistants can barely understand, his "progress" in promoting social justice has coincided with the "progress" of Friedreich's Ataxia.

Now that brings me to the recent discussion about "...it" and excrement and sitting on top of a dung heap, a manure pile, like Job. The discussion of the book's title and its cover is well taken and I suspect Peter is aware of the "good faith" in which these comments and reservations have been made. References to possible legal consequences of the book's proposed content are also to the point and Peter is by no means naive or oblivious about the "context" in which his statements are being made.

But we shouldn't miss Peter's point. Ever since he was

14 he has had to deal with a deeply unsettling reality. How can a person become equipped to deal with what has been, and is, at work in his physiology. Facing that daunting fact has been central to how his instincts have been formed. And though unequipped on that front, he has been able to achieve and equip himself to "keep going" - this is out of all proportion to what he initially expected when he entered TAFE at Frankston, when he transferred to an Arts degree, when he headed for Melbourne University and enrolled in a PhD programme. I might even say that this memorandum is confirmation of the fact.

Barely equipped and yet he has been able to "progress". And there's the rub. And it hurts. In his 6 and a ½ years at his current place of residence Peter has felt that his move from independent living with "home help supports" to Disability Supported Accommodation, has meant regress not progress. The provider is faced with a tragic lack of capacity.

Peter knows that he is lacking the capacity to halt the advance of his Friedreich's Ataxia. But the "provider" of his supported accommodation can't seem to grasp the limits of their organisation's own capacity, or rather incapacity, their own inability. Peter is saying that his experience is shouting at him that Disability Supported Accommodation is in fact making a negative, regressive, contribution if it cannot admit, openly and frankly, that it is ill-equipped to do what it is mandated to do. The honest admission of this inherent limitation in their provision is absent. It thus casts a dark, cruel cloud over their organised efforts to render assistance.

This is a subtle point and it only makes sense when we appreciate just how deep human anguish in suffering can go.

Public policy can make aspirational statements from the glossy documents produced by committees. They can assert that proposed changes will help those unable to move to be mobile in a dynamic society; those unable to speak will finally have their voice heard; those whose muscular energy is being filtered away will be strengthened as valued members of society, and so on. As Peter has written somewhere: such "codes of conduct" for such organisations can too easily become mere "smiley faces" if they are neglecting to breathe in deeply and empathise with the human anguish from which they receive their mandate. This is indeed a sobering political insight. This is basic also to Peter's critique of neo-liberal social policy, a sharpened understanding of how the advertising and marketing of such organisations is cruel and hurtful in its superficialities. That's the problem; that's the dunghill that is problematic for Peter at this stage in his deeply challenging "progress".

BCW

INTRODUCTION

The Structure of This Book

The book develops a series of key themes: looking at the individualistic pursuits of Friedreich's Ataxia; the dignity of risk; analysing neoliberalism; looking at the drivers of disability and their penny-pinching tactics; synergy between support workers in shared support accommodation and the residents like me; a push for justice for people with severe physical disabilities; and a focus on whether disability can hinder you from achieving your goals. Through these steps, the analysis moves from looking at broad social and political ideas and structures, considering the implications for people with disabilities, to looking at specific policy areas.

The different chapters of the book draw on material I have previously published. The evidence, arguments and personal experience are put together here as a collection of essays that illustrate the bigger picture. The book examines many socio-economic and political dimensions of inequality, marginalisation and exclusion – particularly as they affect people with disabilities. It treats these problems as interdependent and cumulative. Hence, the great policy challenge to which I seek to contribute – trying to make a difference.

The general motivation for my book is the belief that we need a better understanding of how to create a genuinely inclusive society. It is not an easy journey, personally or politically, but it is critically important from the perspective of social justice.

CHAPTER 1

"To live is to suffer, to survive is to find some meaning in the suffering."

- Friedrich Nietzsche

Me and the Individualistic Pursuits of Friedreich's Ataxia

I present myself to you as an individual who has been remarkable enough in my own way!

My life, to date, has been unduly constrained by the enforcement of standardised practices, stereotypes and official policies that have been wholly designed to uphold the conclusions of cost–benefit analyses conducted by self-interested disability 'service providers' – the same providers that support people like myself with high-support needs.

Since my diagnosis and the onset of Friedreich's Ataxia 41 years ago, the disease has progressed significantly affecting me in many ways. But the most distressing concern for me personally has been the deterioration of my speech. There is no doubt that every diagnostic implication, every side effect, of this disability, severely impacts my life, but none more so than the important need for me to communicate. Communication is a core necessity, the foundation upon which I attempt to realise my goals.

I have had to struggle with my disability and consequent socio-economic obstacles since I was a teenager. I was 14 years old when diagnosed with Friedreich's Ataxia. It's a progressive disease, causing impairment to the nerves leading to a failure of timely muscle reactions throughout my body. Initially, my only apparent physical abnormality was an uncoordinated gait, not dissimilar to the appearance of someone under the influence of alcohol, but I quickly became expert at hiding such frailties. For whatever reason, I was never without friends, and was never, to my knowledge, made fun of by school friends and peers.

When I was 18 my mother died of cancer. This was a devastatingly emotional time, and my disease temporarily took control, which for me led to a physical and emotional downward spiral. Fortunately, the closeness of family and friends helped ease the pain. They helped me achieve some level of self-esteem and pride in my life. At 18, I was free and able to seek activities and forms of stimulation that were outside the regular activities associated with adolescence. I succumbed to the lure of city-based glitz and glamour, where not everybody appreciated my uniquely uncoordinated style of dancing. I was an easy target for bullies, and on a couple of occasions this developed into trouble.

After a few years of soul searching, I found myself falling in love with a beautiful young nurse, whom I'd met when attending hospital. We ended up living together for about 12 months and became engaged. This experience was fantastic and one that, even now, I miss and continually remember with yearning. Unfortunately, the romance ended six months after our engagement; this break-up was not unrelated to my disability.

To some degree, while we were together but even more so after the relationship with my fiancée ended, I developed a strong desire to pursue further education, and I am grateful for my ex-fiancée's inspiration in that regard. This was the prequel to what has become my miraculous journey with education.

During the 21 years I lived alone, I successfully completed my several academic degrees. First, at the age of 28, I completed an Associate Diploma in Business Studies (Accounting). Then I went to Monash University Peninsula and did a double degree in Arts and Accounting. After that I went to Monash University Clayton for a Master of Arts. And finally, I went to the University of Melbourne, where I successfully completed a Doctor of Philosophy. My PhD was achieved late into the progression of my disease, when I was 43 years old. For me this was a huge achievement, especially when you consider the systemic beliefs among medical practitioners around Friedreich's Ataxia. At the time of my diagnosis, medical specialists told my parents that 'I would not live much beyond the age of thirty', let alone obtain a PhD! These days, I still perform research with the university as an honorary fellow.

With Friedreich's Ataxia, muscle growth is hampered, giving rise to severe deformities, limitations, and a range of other problems. For example, I have had to deal with severe scoliosis (curvature of the spine), and cardiomyopathy (causing a deformed heart). More recently, I am having challenges with my vision and consequently it can take me quite a while to focus. This is especially the case in bright, glary light, which makes it even more difficult. Another challenge for me is nystagmus (blindness).

Friedreich's Ataxia eventually leads to severely slurred speech (dysarthria). By the time I was 40 years old this meant my ability to communicate was seriously impaired, because my speech was incomprehensible. When I finished my PhD I was invited to speak at conferences, but I was never able to directly take up the invitation. Instead, I had someone else read out my papers on my behalf. My inability to communicate also makes it hard for me to socialise, network and build the connections I need within academic circles. Often people think that I have some form of cognitive disability, and consequently treat me accordingly. To overcome this issue, I rely heavily on typing, but this is difficult due to my typing speed, which is often just one to two words a minute.

There has been a strong correlation between my demand for education and my failure to speak properly. My education has compensated for my speech difficulties and has increased my exposure in a fundamental way to options I would not have considered if I had not embarked on further study. In some ways undertaking my education has been something miraculous. But not being able to fully communicate because of my speech impediment has often left me vulnerable to being falsely stereotyped as being cognitively impaired.

Despite these hardships, and during my PhD studies, I received the June Opie Fellowship from Auckland University as well as a Melbourne research scholarship. Immediately after this I was awarded the Emerging Disability Leader of the Year from the Victorian Disability Professionals.

Even though I have achieved so much in academia, the progression of my disability has still been devastating to me in terms of how I am able to involve myself in life, generally. For me, an extremely broad range of life's pursuits are simply beyond my reach. I see this reflected in the field of disability care, where the strengthening of stereotypes lead, to a large degree, the use of standardised processes by the disability care providers who administer care for people like myself.

By 1990, I began to consciously follow my own thoughts and beliefs and to live my own life. By living on my own and receiving the assistance of one-on-one support from workers, I purposely aimed to try my best at becoming and remaining personally responsible. By doing this, my self-esteem received a positive boost that ricocheted and echoed around all other aspects of my life.

Even though these were difficult years, my independence allowed me to have more control over my own affairs. The academic successes I attained while having a severely progressive disability became an integral part of my miraculous journey. By living independently and trying to function on my own terms, as a credible human being, I was forced to speak up for myself. And by doing this I was able to keep at bay my progressively worsening speech impairment.

However, when I turned 49, I moved from living independently into a group facility run by a not-for-profit disability service provider. Initially I accepted this situation, but at the time I was unaware of the practical ramifications that were to follow. I quickly began to feel like I had no control; my individuality and my choices were disregarded by the bureaucracy that ran the shared-support accommodation. Moving into this facility and then being unable to move out has only served to show me that my phenomenal achievements within the education sector actually mean diddley-squat.

Even though I've felt disenfranchised, I've tried to maintain my solidarity for anything and any causes that will enhance my human dignity and development. For me this is a must, but it has been against incredible odds.

Each of the steps I have made through my higher education journey have deepened my desire to promote and harness the capabilities of people who, in diverse ways, are not at all diminished by their disability. I am convinced that, somehow, we – all of us – need to find a way to view and support people with disabilities in proactive and caring ways. Equal opportunity should be a principle for a way of life that is flexible enough to assist diverse disablement in diverse ways. Rather than focusing on combating the uncaring and judgemental stereotypes that arise from the medical model's view of sympathetic charity, we need simply to face up to the diversity of people with severe disabilities as being just that – people. That is, we need a flexible and empathetic approach, aligned to an appreciation of the diverse social abilities, responsibilities, and opportunities that become evident when people interact with each other as fellows, and as equals. This flexible approach to equal opportunity is opposed to many of the conservative voices of meritocracy.

The need for support for my impairment has placed me under constant pressure. That is, I want to be able to function and work at fulfilling my desired needs and wants, but this requires appropriate hours of attendant care. Unfortunately, I am not independently wealthy, and the state system does not provide adequately, in its current form, for all that is required for my particular care.

After my PhD, my options have improved in some ways, but, in reality, I have to ask myself if the cost–benefits involved in pursuing academic excellence are really worth it. Will my degrees give me the necessary skills to pursue my goals of assisting in the provision of a *just and inclusive* society for people with disabilities? Are such pursuits beyond me because of my affliction? Or do my personal narratives identify the political hurdles with greater clarity for others with severe physical disabilities?

CHAPTER 2

Standardisation and Stereotypes

A lack of empathy shown by my service provider, has led me to experience a life over which I have no control during the last six-and-a-half years. Here I am living in a group home where most residents have some form of intellectual disability, yet, we are all standardised and grouped together under one type of disability. When this displacement, or misplacement, is combined with other contextual factors, such as an overworked support staff and to a large degree a system of incompetent management by the service provider, you may begin to sense how I am feeling, which is that my lack of control is now pretty well wall-to-wall chaotic.

Please do not mistake the issue here. It has nothing to do with how my views might be perceived and is all about the individuality of persons living with disability. We are, after all, those who share a diverse humanity, and it may only be our physical or intellectual disability that separates us on some evaluations from a society's so-called norms. What I am concerned about is addressing situations that impede a person's control of life. I want to look at the theories that are capable of addressing the manner in which people's freedom is constrained. Disabled persons are only a special case of persons enduring such unrecognised social constraint.

There is an altruistic consequence of the social service delivery of which I am the beneficiary, namely friendships. At the shared-support accommodation where I now live, which happens to be a workplace albeit in effect 'my place', support workers and people with disabilities become friends, mates even.

But I perceive a problem here and it is a political one.

One of the issues for me is the rapid turnover of staff within the workforce at my shared-support accommodation. Here I would like to make a plea to the disability service provider's management team – please can you resist the casualisation of our workforce. Basic friendships between people with a disability and support workers – like any other relationship – take time to develop. As my body slows, I need to teach my carers how to understand and care for me properly. This sounds simple enough, but I just do not have energy to mount yet another re-education programme every time I get a new support worker. I am asking for sustained consideration at a corporate level about the importance of ensuring work conditions are such that carers can happily stay on caring for us residents. Continuity is so crucial to the ethos of the place.

Today's casualisation of the workforce coincides with the compulsory competitive tendering process that the Department of Health and Human Services (here in Victoria, Australia) requires before granting a contract to run a facility, such as the one where I live. The fear I have is that the residents of disability support service facilities, like myself, are treated too much like commodities for trade when the auctioning season for contract renewal arrives, which, by the way, in turn is followed by the inevitable increase in rent that I am required to pay. I know this sounds extreme, but the tendering process ignores, or misunderstands, the needs of residents to nurture genuine lasting friendships with their carers. The price of friendship is not part of the deal, even though its worth transcends the fair dollar value of the service.

The failure of management to understand this basic principal hollows out the philosophy behind their service delivery, which as a consequence lacks the attributes necessary to provide for the sustained care of residents.

In other words, I am suggesting that the relationship between the support worker and the resident is what this is all about. We cannot deny the relationship factor involved in caring for people with disabilities; we are, after all, humans working closely alongside each other. But the managers of these facilities must acknowledge this if people with disabilities are to gain their full potential and respect in society. This is an industrial issue. We need policies in place to ensure that carers will stay around as an important part of our lives! Sadly, such an insight is foreign to the political horizon of our major parties and the governments they form.

Many parties working in the disability sector fully endorse most of the process of providing individual care for people with disabilities. One of the most profoundly anointed processes is the worldwide benchmark of 'best practice', referred to as 'person-centred planning', where individuals' wants and needs are heeded, they are listened to, and what is important to them is focused on. This creates an ethos of shared power and inclusion.

Delving further into the realities of living in shared-supported accommodation, I would suggest, going by my own experiences, that about 80 per cent of residents have some form of intellectual disability. Therefore, the management of disability service providers who operate shared-support accommodation must cater for this. Understandably, disability service providers favour standardisation of care over the appropriate individual care for people with disabilities in shared-support accommodation. It is cheaper and more efficient, while also allowing for their own self-interested generosity. Without a doubt, the system encourages and enforces the standardisation of disability care. In a nutshell, standardised care may be efficient, but it fails to provide for the individual care of people with disabilities.

Disability service providers, often charity-based organisations, receive generous sums of money for the care of people with disabilities. These payments come in the form of government funding and charitable donations. But within a dysfunctional disability sector these funds often fail to reach their primary target, which is the individual care of people with disabilities, and instead are directed to the top management of these same service providers in the form of excessive wages.

Life becomes extremely complex when people with disabilities are supposed to have their wants and needs provided for with some semblance of respect. From my observations, this is not given.

Terminology that Can Be Standardised and Stereotyped Like Cost and Benefit

Recently, I've been able to witness the demise of fairness within the disability sector – something that has been a harrowing experience for me. I do not feel my individual needs within this shared-support accommodation system have yet been considered, and the seemingly infinite characteristics of any severe disability are yet to be respected. Therefore, for me the standardisation and other efficiencies associated with my care are ridiculous.

An example of the standardised and stereotyping terminology that is used is when, as a resident, I am referred to as a 'customer'.

As a highly intelligent person, in my opinion, as a resident of the facility supported by this service provider, I am certainly NOT a 'customer'. I believe the use of this word in the context of my residency has passed its use-by date. 'Customer' refers to a person who is vulnerable and inadequate. I am already quite well-assured of my vulnerability, in fact I can quite literally feel it in my bones. But am I inadequate? That is what is being questioned by these efficiency policies. Does one have to be a celebrity like the late Stephen Hawking before one can qualify for non-stereotyping?

Branding is another case in point. Does it improve the delivery of service? Yes, branding costs money, and that is OK if it's spent beneficially; however, what often happens is that those extra funds have a tendency to go into the pockets of top management. The costs incurred by service providers with naming and branding can be both negatively and positively exciting; but, whatever the name, or how a new brand looks, it only serves to divert attention from other problems with the functioning of disability service providers.

Am I suggesting that the organisation running the facility where I live should become more political? Yes, I am. But I am also suggesting that they need to do this by emphasising policies that will embody justice and fairness. This way service providers can make a positive contribution not just to the lives of residents and workers, but to wider society and the responsibilities we have as humans for each other.

CHAPTER 3

Notions of Attraction for Some People with Disabilities

Many of the reasons that disability is not attractive from what I would call a 'love interest' sense, arise from baseless stereotypes. These are formed according to an antiquated medical model of what it means to be attractive.

I've already explained, but it is important to keep emphasising, I am not a person with cognitive, behavioural, or developmental disabilities. Moreover, as you can probably understand, I do not take kindly to being treated as if I do have these kinds of disability. Likewise, I am also sure many people with intellectual disabilities do not take kindly to being treated like a semi-paralysed person who must live in a wheelchair. Such mistreatment is a total disregard of a person's humanity, a violation of their rights, and shows a lack of respect.

It is possible, I believe, to eliminate the stereotypical

fears of inadequacy that are not only held by people with severe physical disabilities, but just as importantly are often held by those who 'care' for them. The trick is to encourage the dispirited person with a disability to seek out stories that inspire.

There are many who excel in different walks of life, and who acknowledge the beneficial enrichment of their experiences by those who have such different abilities to their own. Often there is the subsequent development of abilities, and an attraction, which is nothing less than awesome. I had conducted some research into what I prefer to call 'inter-ability relationships', between those depicted as being 'extremely disabled' and those who are not. The results were interesting and heart-warming, to say the least.

One of my most recent research endeavours was to tour the website of Megan (able-bodied) and Barton (severe cerebral palsy), focusing on their marriage and love life. They share a passion to communicate using the written word. Their ability to love and laugh together was initially founded on their mutual passion for writing. Megan and Barton Cutter went on to publish a book, called Ink in the Wheels: Stories to Make Love Roll.

They are unique characters who drive their own story of love and relationship. Love never rolls by itself, and so it is understandable that they've experienced the ups and downs that are present in most relationships. But they've pulled together through this to tell the story of how they faced the challenges of being an 'inter-ability' married couple.

Ink in the Wheels is a phenomenally powerful love story that allows people to understand some of their triumphs that have come about by their sheer determination. With their example as a couple, Megan and Barton Cutter overcome all stereotypes that exist about loving relationships.

Therefore, I would say, don't deny the capacity of people with disabilities to love.

In an attempt to drive home my feelings on this, I will reveal something about myself that I have previously made public, and have already mentioned in this book. In the 41 years since my diagnosis with a severely progressive disability, I have been no stranger to inter-ability relationships, but finding the right person who can handle me and my disability has been difficult.

This experience has been hard enough, but how am I also to deal with the demeaning and deplorable stereotypes held by many in our society? Such attitudes, I believe, make it difficult for me to create, develop and sustain the kind of relationship I want.

I do not have a complete philosophical account of why I enjoy the chance or fulfilment of making love, but I would guess it's as simple as being a case of because I am human. It is also one form of human pleasure that I am still capable of performing. While my physical abilities may be dwindling, and on a consciousness level that is distressing, my ability to love has increased. And for the life of me I don't understand why I also need to combat the utterly ridiculous stereotypes imposed by others upon my being. Despite the dumb thinking and incoherent logical responses given to me in relation to this matter, I reiterate – I don't have a cognitive disability. I should be respected for my intellect and my knowledge, as should all people with disabilities be similarly respected for their differences and individual perspectives.

Like many stereotypes, this perception is to some degree an inescapable societal reality, however, it is also the fulfilment of social misguidance.

Is society changing? Is there more acceptance of differences in 'love' these days as it is publicly discussed? The answer is yes, but the debate still has a long way to go. This is not to forget that there is also a need for ongoing redemption from past mistakes.

CHAPTER 4

Dignity of Risk Should be a Disability Right

There is a concept called 'dignity of risk'. This refers to the right of everyone to pursue activities that have a level of risk such as, for example, going swimming or surfing. However, the risk in those examples can be managed by checking the conditions before going, or going with a friend. Does this mean that a disability service provider or the carer of someone with a disability has to assume responsibility on that person's behalf by balancing the risk to the disabled person and the right of that person to pursue happiness? I would suggest that people with disabilities are usually in the best position to decide their own acceptable level of risk and to instruct their own support services. Dignity of risk should mean that support services encourage people with disabilities to make their own informed choices.

Stereotyping and discriminatory attitudes can make it difficult for a person with disabilities to be a 'normal person'. It follows that the disabled person should decide for him or herself what their own 'dignity of risk' level is. Recognition of this need will facilitate a better relationship between the support workers and the disabled.

The danger is that the principle of 'dignity of risk' is something that can be overridden, and as a result the disabled person's support turned into a legal tug of war. Sometimes people with a disability are prevented from making certain decisions or participating in activities because other people judge these to be too risky. How risk is perceived is unique to each of us as individuals, and management of any risk should be tailored to a person's individual circumstances. In the following section I give an example where my own right to the dignity of risk was overridden.

Standardising and the Need for an Individualised Approach

When I lived in my own home, I used a sling to move myself from place to place. When I moved into shared-support accommodation six-and-a-half years ago I was told that it did not meet their 'standards'. It was explained to me that another person using this sling had died and therefore it was deemed unsafe. Full stop. Never mind that I had successfully used the sling for 15 years.

Disability services should be encouraged to avoid processes that standardise disabilities. Each person needs to be understood and respected on his or her own terms. I've had 15 years' experience with my sling and I should have been allowed to demonstrate its features, and how it posed no great risk for me.

I was only allowed to enter this new house after a total rearrangement of most of my equipment, much of which I had been using for many years. All of a sudden my equipment was dispensed with because it, apparently, did not meet the safety standards of the new house. Standard procedure is one thing, but care in supporting those with disability ought not to be neglected in the process. This aspect of my move cost me a great deal of money as well as causing me much emotional turmoil.

The Potential of Synergy as a Way Forward for the Disability Sector

Consider the dynamics of mutually beneficial partnerships between attendant carers and the people they care for – people who rather than being merely disabled should be viewed as those with many different abilities. This exploration considers some pragmatic examples, which encourage the participation of these people in contributing to a more inclusive society.

The underlying goal of mutually beneficial partnerships is to chart the further education of those directly and indirectly related to disability work. The aim is to identify pathways that are courteous, mutually beneficial and helpful. The pathway needs to be identified so that, by travelling it together, both parties can truly share life together. The potential benefits for developing such mutually beneficial partnerships are substantial. The flow-on will be to all those in society who are indirectly and directly affected by disability. For example, there is an unlimited possibility for the transference of abilities, which will create a new potential for people with different abilities and support workers in a dynamic, merit-based society.

The synergistic outcomes that can flow from this form of flexible support can be demonstrated through my own (unpaid) work. Synergy is a term that is popular in most human resource management departments. Simply defined, it means that the whole is greater than the sum of its parts: that is, 1+1=3. In my case the synergistic partnership between my support worker and myself allows me to shine in my role as a disability activist.

The synergy that is provided to me through the intervention of flexible disability support provides me with the means to achieve many of my goals in life. This approach to personal care is cohesive, flexible, and humane. It allows me to manage the complexities of my life and desires. It helps me to attain my full human potential when and where my bodily abilities are lacking. For example, despite the deterioration of motor skills, I am still able to perform research and write articles at a significant rate beyond that of many paid workers in the disability sector. My performance is created through the synergy gained mainly through the effort of my support worker.

This synergy explains the transformation that takes place in people with such different abilities and their support workers, where the mutual benefits that occur provide for a more proficient and humanly thoughtful disability sector, and for a more inclusive society. Synergy becomes a fundamentally conscious event that motivates, transforms and unifies all of life with concerted and organised combinations of those with different abilities and support workers. This then, in my view, is the path to unify and enhance the disability sector.

Synergy for people with different abilities and support workers is about life chances and the creation of opportunities. Therefore, the essence of synergy is to value difference.

Consider these thoughts of Christina Irugalbandara, my current academic support worker.

> My name is Christina Irugalbandara, a student from Monash University. I have been directly em-

ployed as an academic support worker for Peter Gibilisco. I assist Peter with computer-based administrative and academic tasks, particularly in relation to his articles, blog posts and this book. Together with Peter's immense knowledge and my abilities, we can generally produce fast, efficient and improved results, as documented in this book. Peter has a lot of intelligence and expertise in the field of his study, but his abilities to put his thoughts to words is restricted by the debilitating side-effects of his disability. However, with my assistance, he can get his thoughts on paper at the rate of 50 words a minute.

'Nothing About Us Without Us'

In highlighting the need for synergistic procedures to take place, I am reminded of a motto that should be proclaimed loud and clear across Australia's disability sector. This motto is about disability. It says this: 'Nothing about us without us'. Think about it. I am concerned that too many professionals in the disability sector act as if they do not even consider this, let alone take it to heart. Why have those who wield power in the disability sector failed to advocate this idea more strongly? We might say the same thing of my pragmatic ideas listed above. Those at work in the disability sector need to find ways to enable themselves to be active advocates of this basic democratic idea.

CHAPTER 5

Neoliberalism and People with Disabilities

"A silly political scientist comes to economics convinced that all relations are basically power relations, and most power relations are organized as class relations, so economists should simply study the system of economic power. By contrast, a sensible political scientist comes to economics with an alert eye for the possibility of different market strengths, including different political or legal advantages, in the parties to market bargains: i.e. with some additional questions to ask, or some scepticism about the economists' conceptions of market relations - and also with questions about the actual patterns of business or labor or green or feminist or consumers' influence on the makers of public economic policy.

Theory can often point to the need for research. But privileged theory, including neoclassical economic theory, becomes dangerous when it denies the need for research by asserting what always happens, so must be happening in any particular case."

- Hugh Stretton

Politics has changed so much over the years; our political climate is unstable. Since 2007 we have had five different prime ministers in Australia. You might well ask, how then, does this affect people with severe physical disabilities?

Neoliberalism is a political economic theory and practice that has emerged with greater and greater appeal since the 1960s, and since the 1980s it has increased in prominence at the level of public policy formulation. The aim of neoliberalism, a form of liberalism that favours free-market capitalism, is to question all collective structures capable of obstructing the logic of the pure market. Such a belief allows one to question the ideology behind the welfare state, behind progressive taxation, and other social policies that can lead to an egalitarian society. The neoliberalist ideology harvests the sentiment that many welfare recipients are lazy and should do more to help grow the economy. Neoliberals are persistently oriented towards supporting a society in which self-interest prevails and that is why they give all their energy to policies that claim to further the individual pursuit of wealth. That is, the individual pursuits that are deemed worthy of government support are those that are beyond those living on the 'other side' of the great divide between the rich and the poor.

Individual pursuits, whether of the rich or the poor, are just about always justified in terms of one's self-interest. This goes a long way to explaining the dogmatic reasoning behind the powerful ideology as it is supported by the very rich. It is also confirmed by the equally dogmatic phrase: 'power is money'.

Liberal political and economic policies are dominated by this ideological viewpoint. Such policies have been integral to political economies all over the world, in both developed and developing countries. The rebirth of liberalism as neoliberalism was seen as the answer to the western world's problem of stagflation, which reared its head in the mid-1970s. Hugh Stretton put it well:

> Alternative strategies for dealing with the offending stagflation would advantage different classes, parties, industries. Economic reform was as usual a political task. Other interests saw opportunities to change the direction of development to improve the mixed economies' efficiency by means which would incidentally make the rich richer, business freer, welfare cheaper and the poor more self-reliant. Those means were described as de-regulating, privatising, restoring competition, cutting welfare, 'rolling the boundaries of government' (Stretton, 1986:7).

The neoliberal approach rejects social democratic doctrines. Neoliberalism focuses politically on the establishment of a stable medium of exchange, the reduction of localised rules, regulations and barriers to free-ranging commerce, and the privatisation of state-run enterprises. This contemporary and dominant economic ideology of most western countries is referred to with a 'neo' prefix, because it is a latter-day version of the classical liberalism that initially arose in the 18th century. Moreover, neoliberalism claims to be a political system designed to highlight both the political limitations of the market economy in the nation-state, and the economic efficiency and effectiveness of the market economy when it is freed to operate on a global scale.

The theory of classical liberal economics was developed by Adam Smith, the Scottish economist, philosopher and author, and we can sense its appeal at what we now say was the beginning of Great Britain's Industrial Revolution (around 1760). Smith argued that government intervention disrupted the natural order of society, which, according to Smith, can be defined as a society left to its own devices. Smith based his economic beliefs on the argument that most economic self-interest is altruistic.

According to Smith, this classical liberal system would provide for an economic infrastructure that could not only bestow economic benefits, but also help promote a proud, virtuous and motivated society. I will display the mixed emotions of self-interest through a simple philosophical scenario. In this scenario, two individuals, a stranger and a local, have a conversation. The stranger, who needs to go to the local council, is directed by the local in the direction of the post office, because the local needs his letter posted. The stranger accepts the letter and goes his way, but not before opening it to see if there is something valuable inside.

During an interview with me, Hugh Stretton explained his dissent from this ideological interpretation of Adam Smith. He pointed out that Smith never said that the interests that prompted people's economic decisions and behaviour were all selfish. Smith's first book, The Theory of Moral Sentiments was about our feelings, and concerns about other people's needs, safety and happiness, as well as our own. When he said, in The Wealth of Nations, that he owed his breakfast to his baker's self-interest, there is good reason to think that Smith meant the baker's joy in his skills and work, and pride in the quality of his bread and the pleasure it could give his bread's consumers, as well as the money it earned him.

Now, after thinking about this for some years, I come to the view that something like this principle is working itself out in my own relationship with what is now referred to as the 'disability sector'.

As it is commonly understood, selflessness is a principle or practice of concern for the welfare of others. But my situation seems to be endorsed by Smith. In the social service delivery involving a personal-care attendant – of which I am a recipient – the 'altruistic' effects that work themselves out in the workplace become a friendship circle – where the workers and their clients are mates. Consider this: the workplace of the disability support worker is actually our home in which the residents actively welcome visitors to their 'space', under their private 'roof'. It is not only those who are paid for their work in this workplace who have an interest, a general self-interest, in forming what takes place. After all it is also a place sustained by the friendships that are generated there.

Smith certainly believed that people's generous feelings, and concern for others' safety and prosperity as well as their own could join in determining their market choices and their social and political values and behaviour. Because it comes from the neoliberal 'bible' (Smith's *The Wealth of Nations*) I think this observation must play a vital part of any effective attack on the neoliberals' assumption that material self-interest is the sufficient cause of market efficiency, which in turn, they then suggest, is a necessary condition – many even think of it as a sufficient condition – of a good society.

More than 20 years ago Hugh Stretton, in his book *Political Essays*, told of a 'Cult of Selfishness' that spoke of the emergence of neoliberalism that now provides us with significant cultural hindsight.

This is further acknowledged in the Australian government's (ALP) *Shut Out* report – a broad government publication of issues confronting people with disabilities:

> The extraordinary gap between the level of income support and the cost of disability was seen as restricting the ability of people with disabilities both to live independently and to enjoy a decent standard of living... Disability support recipients

> live lives of fear and desperation. Sooner or later every disability support recipient I know has confessed to the concern they feel over the 'what if' factor – what if government stops paying social security/disability support?

What is Equal Opportunity?

Meritocracy

Meritocracy is a belief that seems to me to still be alive and well in the senior management of disability support services. It also seems to drive many aspects of public policy, particularly when appeals are made to equal opportunity.

Advocates of a meritocratic approach to disability policy are still assuming that the base-line principle should be that people get out of the system what they put into it. That is why they seek to remove any barriers to people with disabilities 'putting in'. It is a political vision – often articulated in terms of free-market principles – that wants a future based on merit. Hence meritocracy (rule by those who gain merit) is an alternative to aristocracy (the rule by those who inherit land), or more recently to a class based on the luck of being born in the right place at the right time. But in 1998 in an article titled 'Meritocracy Revisited', Michael Young (a British sociologist, social activist and politician who coined the term 'meritocracy', 1915–2002) argued, meritocracy is even worse than aristocracy because it assumes power and privilege as merited as opposed to inherited.

Young has a negative view of meritocracy. His 1958 book titled *The Rise of Meritocracy* was a satire (meaning a system based on merit has unforeseen consequences that will eventually make mobility from one place in the social system to another even more restricted). In recent years he has felt compelled to criticise 'new Labour' because of its meritocratic commitment as advocated by the policies of Third Way of the Tony Blair Labour Government in the UK (1998–2007). Anthony Giddens, the renowned political academic and Blair supporter, argues that any meritocratic equity is flawed, creating deep inequalities of outcome that threatens social cohesion. Likewise, Roy Hattersley, British Labour Party MP, was of the view that meritocracy only offers shifting patterns of inequality, unfairly exalting the rich, while condemning the poor to false hopes of individualised social mobility.

My argument is that, public policy with respect to the involvement of people with disability in mainstream society must be as much about affirmative action as it is with equal opportunity.

So what kind of affirmative action am I proposing?

My Requirements for Affirmative Action

I am the beneficiary of a higher education system that has been required by law to make room for people with disabilities like myself. But it needs to be remembered that such requirements were put in place in a context where higher education was re-oriented, making it compatible with job training for a post-industrial society. The acquisition of a university degree may seem to be evidence that people with disabilities have been given an equal opportunity to compete, but when I think about my own life and experience I conclude that for equal opportunity to be a reality, affirmative action has to be taken to a new level. By necessity this will involve a totally new understanding of 'mutual obligation'.

What do I mean? We need universities that will recognise their mutual obligation to contribute is institutional and is not simply a matter of granting space in courses to individuals. That obligation is not completed merely by granting degrees and then every year thereafter sending out brochures inviting such highly qualified alumni (including disabled alumni) to give generously to the university's noble cause. Such brochures might feature people in wheelchairs dressed up for graduation, but my point is if that is all the university's mutual obligation means, they are simply in the game of turning disabled graduates into celebrities!

In future, when severely disabled students get as far as I was lucky to get, I hope universities can give space to ensure graduates can indeed 'give back' as part of post-doctoral and ongoing research programmes. What I am concerned about is the development of genuine policy for the severely disabled and in particular policies that seek to meet needs that arise from progressive disability.

For example, my disability, Friedreich's Ataxia, is a chronic disease that will severely worsen over time (it is a progressive disability). Meanwhile, medical practitioners espouse treatments that promote the idiom, 'if you don't use it, you lose it'. Such an ideology suggests that to help improve deteriorating coordination, medical action is needed to strengthen the muscles. Somehow, assistance for those with progressive conditions – such as people like myself with Friedreich's Ataxia – is needed if they are to gain some 'elbow room' in life. This simply affirms the importance of ongoing medical research, not just to keep people alive but to assist in the social and public contributions of people with progressive debilitations.

What I'm trying to articulate is the importance of developing a 'medical research consciousness' that tackles the need to help people with Friedreich's Ataxia and similar progressive conditions find ways of gaining work-related skills, as well as ways to help sustain those skills for as long as possible. In my opinion, and based on my own research, there is no doubt that correctly applied affirmative action can deliver appropriate opportunities for people with severe and progressive disabilities enabling them to have a go at life.

In my view, it is the political economy driven by a radical free-market agenda that is a fundamental source of the problems faced by people with disabilities. The theoretical problem faced by researchers like myself, as we seek to clarify our critique and set forth alternative policy, is to show how the problems faced by people with disabilities are directly related to prejudicial or discriminatory attitudes.

The market-driven system routinely puts profits before people's well-being, so when employers are faced with 'equal opportunity' demands for employment they will characteristically assume that they will have to make room for lowered productivity, higher costs and greater hurdles to workplace efficiency (when employing severely disabled graduates). The point is that a small business may have an owner who is very sympathetic but who will go to the wall if margins are not properly managed.

Affirmative Action

It is necessary, then, to look again at what is meant by 'affirmative action' legislation. This political and policy approach requires constructive steps to promote and maintain equal employment opportunity for socially defined (in terms of gender, disability, age, and race) population groups whose participation rates are reduced or non-existent due to what might be called 'structural factors'. The legislation stipulates that active steps be taken to promote equal opportunity. It is not just about compliance with the (anti-discrimination) legislation that seeks to eliminate unequal treatment of individuals; the goal of affirmative action is to eliminate disadvantage for anyone enduring discrimination in the workforce at any workplace for which they cannot be held responsible. Affirmative action programmes seek to appeal to an entire polity's responsibility to counter the impacts of any 'structural discrimination' upon socially defined groups. Thus, affirmative action requires employers to take active steps to provide equal employment opportunities for groups subjected to discrimination in employment.

Frank Stilwell and other advocates of affirmative action also argue that it is about much more than merely a redistribution of income. It is about life chances. People with disabilities often experience the contraction of their life chances simply because unjustified stereotypes are not put to the test of a truly critical examination. Their life chances are often already diminished, so to challenge the stereotype seems to require a change of cosmic proportions. However, legally enforceable affirmative action for people with disabilities can mandate that a certain percentage of positions must be filled by employees with disabilities.

Still, it should be noted that this approach has challenges, not only from the private sector and from government, but also from within the disability rights movement itself. There is a deep suspicion that an unanticipated consequence of affirmative action will be the promotion of discriminatory stereotypes and stigmas within the workforce. Are people with disabilities to be hired merely because it is regulated that employers do so? Can a campaign mandating a 'politically correct' attitude eradicate discriminatory stereotypes? In the long run, it is assumed that this legally enforceable political correctness will promote the employment of people with disabilities as a societal norm.

The neoliberal elements in the disability movement decided that all we needed was an 'equal opportunity', as opposed to affirmative action to remedy past patterns of discrimination. It would definitely be revolutionary for corporations to hire us, and to prevent corporations from firing employees upon disablement. Affirmative action may be only incrementalist reform – which admittedly does not solve the question of full employment – but it has gotten some results for other minorities.

This is opportunity, in terms of its anti-discrimination focus, with the competitive market system creating a regulated need for affirmative action.

That is, a person with a disability's theoretical right to a public accommodation is really no right at all; it is still dependent upon the employer's cost–benefit analysis. In private business, the bottom line is to accumulate profits and pay the costs involved in making them. The political economic context of free-market capitalism, and the promotion of the market by neoliberal and Third-Way policy, provides a significant obstacle to the implementation of affirmative action policies.

Mutual Obligation

'Mutual obligation' was a political buzzword during Prime Minister John Howard's leadership from 1996 to 2007. The political definition of the term is that 'mutual obligation is based on a concept that welfare assistance provided to the unemployed of working age should involve some return responsibilities for the recipient'.

With my own coherent thoughts, I feel despair and frustration at every level. At every stage of life's pursuits, I have desperately tried to better myself and society to the best of my abilities. I have done so through my academic achievements. And, yes, in comparison to society's norm, there has been a failure to understand that my academic success and contributions as a disability advocate are a form of mutual obligation.

Therefore, it can be said that I have played my part with the hand that I have been dealt.

Upon graduating with my PhD in 2006, important people told me a self-motivating statistical fact: that is, only 1 per cent of people worldwide have successfully completed a PhD. However, for me, life after my PhD became more difficult. My life was my own, but it was extremely constrained by the fact that now I had a PhD, but I had no job, no money, and very little chance of ever obtaining a professional position that matches my qualifications. OK, I may never starve, but there is more to life than just getting from one meal to the next. How can I achieve anything in both a body that restricts my movements, and a society that does not value my achievements?

In my previous book, *The Politics of Disability*, I put it like this:

> *In 2007, I was presented with the Emerging Disability Leader Award. I also applied for many positions after graduating, after being 'doctored'. I am confident that I could have performed well in many of these positions, but I was unable to secure employment. The constraints that are assumed from a neoliberal economic perspective mean that even not-for-profit firms find it difficult to employ people like myself. I believe I know how to make a contribution that could improve or*

> *at least maintain viability of the services offered by such firms. But to this day my 'mutual obligation in public service' is channelled through positions which can never allow me the active social inclusion that regular employment would provide.*

I believe that with my PhD, had I been given the opportunity, I would have been able to challenge the hard-edge facts about the progression of Friedreich's Ataxia. Instead, I spent most of the last six-and-a-half years in shared-support accommodation, which has to a large degree improperly imprisoned my life. I look back on these years and feel unfairly shoved aside and psychologically burdened with a sense of my own loss of control. It was in July 2011 when I moved into a group home for people with high-support needs that I started experiencing a progressive sense of a loss of control (which is detrimental to, and influences biomedical conditions such as Friedreich's Ataxia). There are depressing side-effects associated with this loss of control, particularly with regards to the social effects of Friedreich's Ataxia, not unlike the neurological loss of muscular power.

Why do I deserve mutual obligation? The development of my education has not been viewed by the wider community as a substantial contribution to society because of the stigmas surrounding my disability, the disutility of employers, and the lack of employment opportunities I have been given.

All this brings me to the NDIS. My disability is so profound and challenging that now I cannot do even the most basic of tasks such as, for example, feeding myself. Even wheeling my chair around is impossible to do on my own. Most importantly, with my speech, I am finding it difficult to convey my meaning with even basic words. There are only a handful of people who can understand me because they are familiar with my speech. You can see, then, this comes back to the constant changeover of support staff in shared-support accommodation, which is detrimental to my well-being.

Speech deterioration is something that can be helped to a certain extent by involving myself in everyday conversation, but in the living environment where I am housed it becomes a problematic, complex situation because of the standardisation of residents' speech and other communications. This situation creates pain and stress for me, and another hurdle when it comes to me being able to make future contributions.

My need for constant care is something that cannot be logically undertaken in shared-support accommodation. I have always done whatever I could in life; the most notable achievement being the pursuit of my education from the ages of 28 to 43, the time when I experienced severe progression of my Friedreich's Ataxia.

The federal government has the ability to do more for me, and for others in my situation.

The National Disability Insurance Scheme (NDIS): A Personal View

I look back on the last six-and-a-half years, since July 2011 when I moved into a group home for people with high-support needs and come to a sad conclusion. For some considerable time, I have been losing control of my ability to move. But, in addition to that, from that time there has occurred a progressive loss of control more fundamental than the physiological and biological loss of muscular power – that is the loss of my social and personal powers.

Various people encouraged my move into shared-care accommodation. The Department of Human Services, as it was then known, was unable to allocate me a support worker for an extra three hours a day. Those three hours were necessary for me to be able to work safely and productively during the day in my own residence.

At no stage did I envisage the kind of loss of control over my life that I have subsequently experienced – in a personal and social sense – nor was the possibility of this brought to my attention by those encouraging me to make this decision, not least those in charge of the facility in which I have subsequently found myself. The 'movers and the shakers' in disability care, those who are stakeholders in the disability care industry, seek to find a solution that is cheap and safe for people with a disability, rather than a solution that provides a flexible supportive regime that maintains the good things that have previously been a part of an already constrained life.

Hopefully, though, life may be much better under the NDIS. The NDIS has a social platform that rests on the provision of control, social empowerment, and understanding.

Please do not mistake the issue here. It has nothing to do with how my views might be perceived and is all about the individuality of persons living with disabilities. We are, after all, those who share a diverse humanity, and it may only be our physical or intellectual disability that separates us from society's so-called norms. What I am concerned about is addressing situations that impede a person's control of their own life. I want to look at theories capable of addressing the manner in which people's freedom is constrained. Disabled people are only one such special case of people who are enduring this kind of unrecognised social constraint.

The NDIS scheme is based on the view that control and choice about funding provided to people will be individually driven. This means an important shift in the power away from the government and service providers and into the hands of people with disabilities themselves and, of course, their families.

Self-managed funding gives flexibility over the choice of support workers, including with any negotiations about salaries, the hours and the kind of work that is required. As hours of duty and pay rates become more flexible, this may be more attractive to support workers, too. As the employer of one's own support workers, the person with a disability, or their family or trustee, need to be familiar with a range of things, including WorkCover and taxation laws. This can be complicated; the recipient of NDIS needs to ensure they are compliant with all legal, financial and human resource obligations, as well as maintaining employees' records.

Payments from NDIS are based on three different support categories:

- CORE – enabling a participant to complete daily living activities and to work towards their goals and meet their objectives.

- CAPITAL – for investing in, for example, assistive technologies, equipment and home or vehicle modifications, and funding for capital costs (for example, to pay for specialist disability accommodation).

- CAPACITY BUILDING – enabling a participant to build their independence and skills.

A large amount of money is put into the training of disability professionals, but there is little credit given to the ability of people with disabilities, who often act in management roles, for the day-to-day management of their home-based support workers or the management of disability professionals. The people being served here have, in fact, become front-line trainers.

Self-managed support is based on the belief that the people being supported are, more often than not, the best teachers regarding the support they need and how it can be delivered. Self-management is supposed to ensure that financial control of the supports being used is in the hands of people with disabilities, or their family or a trustee. Therefore, social participation in this instance provides individual control and empowerment.

To be a self-manager of your funding is not the only way that you can gain choice and control in the scheme. Every participant of the NDIS has the choice and control over how their funds are managed, including who provides their supports and how these supports are carried out. This is irrespective of whether they choose to self-manage their own funds or get a third party to do this for them.

This flexibility is vital, especially for those who are not capable of managing their own funds or for those who choose not to. Participants with an intellectual disability or with severe psychosocial disability, for example, may find difficulty in managing the specific duties pertaining to the financial side of their plan. Having your funding managed by agencies such as the Plan Management Agency – not the service provider – is just as important as the choice to self-manage. Moreover, parts of the plan may be managed in different ways based on the needs of the individual.

The NDIS is structured on the insurance model, providing social inclusion through an insurance scheme, the goal of which is to achieve better outcomes for people with disabilities. This is so that social programmes are met and empowerment is encouraged. This is quite different from the welfare provision model, and the opposite of its short-term, needs-based structure. It provides insurance instead of welfare. That is, it looks to enhance opportunities instead of looking solely and abstractly at the first-hand, obvious needs. It was because of this utilitarian outlook that many welfare recipients ended up being stereotyped.

The insurance scheme approach to supporting people is different. Built into its approach is a prudential insurance governance cycle that deals with a set of forecasts of what the NDIS will cost. For this, data will be collected that will validate or change those forecasts.

Presently, with the available data about people with disabilities, service providers are able to assess their needs better. And so, they will be able to demonstrate the most effective supports for them, and will be able to assess if the outcomes differ from expectations resulting from the services provided. They can then make changes accordingly. Insurance schemes are data-driven processes. This means that over time it will lead to better, more cost-effective outcomes for people with disabilities and their families.

Welfare schemes aim to minimise costs over very short periods of time, whereas insurance schemes minimise costs and maximise opportunities over a person's lifetime and are more aligned to an individual's needs. Therefore, the NDIS will reap better outcomes as it invests in independence and participation of individuals and the nurturing relationships of their families and loved ones. It also holds out the prospect of the nurturing of these vital relationships by all involved.

In addition to being data-driven, the NDIS invests in research, for example, accident compensation schemes have been researched thoroughly. Insurance companies have been important sources of social change as it gives the wider community the opportunity to pool in their money towards the amelioration of the lifestyle of people with disabilities. And so, this will ultimately lead to greater social outcomes including a reduction in attitudes based on stereotypes.

CHAPTER 6

The Drivers Behind Disability, and the Penny-Pinching Tactics Behind Shared-Support Accommodation

---

> "The social model of disability is a reaction to the dominant medical model of disability which in itself is a functional analysis of the body as machine to be fixed in order to conform with normative values. The social construction of disability is the idea that society and its institutions have the power to construct disability around social expectations of health. The social model of disability identifies systemic barriers, negative attitudes and exclusion by society (purposely or inadvertently) that mean society is the main contributory factor in disabling people. While physical, sensory, intellectual, or psychological variations may cause individual function-

al limitation or impairments, these do not have to lead to disability unless society fails to take account of and include people regardless of their individual differences."

- Wikipedia

Realigning the Social Model for a Better Understanding of Disability

My life has been significantly challenged and soured by a disability that has diluted all aspects of it. How do you value disability, at the same time as mourn the loss of ability? That is, most political movements are founded on the demand to overturn injustices (righting wrongs) – and the disability movement is no different.

For people with disabilities to gain a natural 'tenancy' within life and to discover its normal conquests at each stage of the life process, a social movement must demonstrate that the goal for an inclusive future is no idealistic dream. To do this it needs to gain and harness media support through the promotion of life stories that illustrate how people with disabilities are capable of initiating these 'normal' pathways. Such a movement should promote the life stories of people with disabilities who have succeeded. And so, when stories of people with disabilities succeeding in life become a natural part of everyday existence, a movement grows. More stories are brought to light because people begin to see the possibilities.

Of course, the first step towards unwinding any entrenched resistance towards people with disabilities' rightful access to the opportunities that are freely available to others must be to promote positive images, and to excavate the hidden history of great contributions, of heroic stories, and of how efforts have been made to move towards light and glory. We need to assert our right to exist.

People with disabilities are among the world's most political and socioeconomically downtrodden. Together, disability and social injustice have created monstrous evil. Jenny Cooper in *Inclusion is our Destiny* wrote:

> During the witch hunts of medieval times, millions

> of disabled people were put to death as witches. The catalogue of crimes continued in the nineteenth century with the 'Eugenicist' movement attempted to improve the quality of the human race by selective breeding. Disabled people were shut away in separate institutions and sterilised. Coinciding as it did with the growth of competing European empires, each wanting to prove superiority, this ultimately led to the murder of 140,000 disabled adults and 100,000 children at the hands of the Third Reich in Nazi Germany.

Throughout history, we must admit that a basic contempt for people with disabilities has prevailed at the forefront of what has been said to be 'progress'. But today we stand on the edge of a new political era; globalisation should mean that human rights have top priority.

Personally, as I have experienced the gradual progression of my disease, I have deepened in my understanding of how exclusion from social life arises as if it is simply normal. At the same time, by being motivated by the hope of better times to come, I have engaged and succeeded in the academic world.

As I will argue, social policy has developed so that many people with disabilities can now attempt and possibly achieve their goals. They can do so with less harassment from unjustified stereotypes and discrimination. Ideally, a socially deepened understanding of disability could stop most forms of discrimination against people with disabilities.

This is not to misjudge or de-emphasise the situation of empowering people with disabilities. We should not be complacent. Yes, much has been done, but there is still further to go.

Let me try to explain what I suspect is needed to further the disclosure of rights for people with disabilities. Today, disability is typically studied in two ways. The first is the medical model of disability, which looks at disability as a medical illness that either: has to be cured medically (by medicine or medical procedures and technological assistance) at an individual level; or controlled (by various technological devices or a prosthetic aid) to allow the person with a disability to become a normal functioning member of society.

On the other hand, there is the social model of disability that understands disability to be the outcome of social, political and economic processes, which have an impact on the lives of people identified as disabled, as well as on the lives of people who are not identified as disabled.

Whereas the medical model focuses on the individual as a patient, by contrast, the social model focuses on the infinite social processes and dynamics of disability. The social model is empathetic to the view that discrimination and prejudice around disability is made stronger by a lack of accessible, socially and economically rewarding information, a lack of suitable technology and events, and inadequate architecture.

The antiquated view of the medical model has created persistent stereotypes and a resultant stigma for people with disabilities. The adherents to the medical model believe that people with disabilities may never attain acceptable social norms without a complete cure. This leaves those who cannot be cured with an impossible dilemma leading to their social, economic, political and cultural marginalisation. While the care and support given to people with disabilities has increased over recent years, I'm concerned by the trend towards standardising disability services. In order to realise the infinite possibilities of individuals with a disability, support must be provided on an individual basis.

My own experience reveals the failure of the medical model of disability. For others and for me it has been a source of stigma and discrimination. I have been pitied, conveniently verbally misunderstood, looked down on for my supposed abnormal structure and characteristics, and regarded as a loser.

The social model of disability, by contrast, challenges this stigma and discrimination. The social model has the potential to roll back societal prejudice and misguidance, and to support people with disabilities in their attempts to possibly achieve their goals free of harassment, stereotypes and discrimination.

I believe, the social exclusion of people with disabilities occurs because most people are still operating using the medical model of disability. They have not been exposed to the social model.

My life, to a large degree, has been structured in accordance with the social model of people with disabilities. I had felt no reason to place any belief in the ideas put forward by the medical model that would view me as somehow inferior because I could not achieve what is considered to be 'normal' in my bodily movements. I see my successful completion of a PhD as proof of the veracity of the social model of disability. But more than ever, I am swayed to a certain degree by realistic and pragmatic medical opinion. Is it because today I can now identify with a future?

Today I am 55-years-old. I have completed a PhD, which is usually considered to be a high honour for even the most able-bodied of persons. I am sure that there will be some recognition of the achievement, but some will plainly refer to it as a novel achievement, or even an illusion that has been created by some creative civil libertarians to further the need for social policy.

While there are severe limitations to the medical model, it is the case that most medically diagnosed impairments will require continued medical support. Medical doctors, medicines and therefore the medical model of treatment, all have a positive impact on the lifestyles of people with disabilities as they should. In this regard, the medical model should not be completely discounted.

For example, some years ago, around 1987, a friend of mine, also with Friedreich's Ataxia, was to be married to the guy of her dreams – an able-bodied individual. As she signed the register, she got too excited, had a heart attack and died. In hindsight, the wedding was a beautiful moment, and the embodiment of the social model. But what should have been done diagnostically, to prevent the heart attack, certainly remains within the medical model. In other words, it is the interaction between the medical and social models of disability that is important. The problems I am talking about arise when the medical model displaces the social model.

To affirm what many people with severe disability think that is I'm not disabled and proud, I'm disabled and pissed off! particularly when the medical model of disability prevails. Still, I want to affirm that hope rises within parts of the social model of disability.

Hugh Stretton has identified what he argues is the need for people to maintain the correct balance between the medical and social models of disability, if people with disabilities are to achieve a rewarding quality of life.

That is, in all aspects of life it is necessary to try to keep the correct balance for success and happiness in all pursuits. The correct balance will assist people with disabilities make necessary choices about how and what to do in life. It is important for people with disabilities to create their lives around what they can do, not what they cannot. For example, today within the higher education sector I feel appreciated, and this has a flow-on effect to many other parts of my life.

To succeed in today's society, most actions by people with disabilities need adequate collective assistance that can best be brought together by means of state assistance. And only on rare occasions are such collective state-empowered actions driven solely by either the social or medical models of people with disabilities.

In the final analysis, we are humans and are therefore simply too complex to rely upon actions that are suggested or sustained by just one political approach or model.

Wherever we may be located within the flow-charts of such organisations, we are all human with our own individual pursuits of happiness. When it comes to high-support needs for people with disabilities, love is not part of the medical model's contribution. It is something that is beyond its control when it comes to meeting the needs of disability. But hopefully it will be there as the indispensable motor of any positive medical contribution. At times, a person with a disability will require more than just physical support in medical, dietary and psychological terms. That is, we need to promote communities of people who consciously function in ways that humanise the clinical methodology of the medical model, and this can be done by giving greater attention to what I would thereby call 'the social model'.

If there is to be any emphasis on the social model of disability support, it will be necessary to emphasise again and again that society is a network of coinciding and interdependent responsibilities.

CHAPTER 7

Customers in Our Own Homes

"Are people with disabilities just passive recipients of care? This is what the term 'customer' implies."

- Christina Irugalbandara

Disability service providers like to standardise all residents as 'customers'. This word has developed a spurious meaning, allowing residents in shared-supported accommodation to be easily stereotyped, or standardised, for the cost–benefit outcomes of service providers. The term 'customer' relates to all residents living in shared-supported accommodation, regardless of their individual disability. The fact is, all disabilities are not the same, as they all have individual aspects and characteristics.

Should the management of shared-supported accommodation stereotype all their residents as one, despite the different types of severe disability, each with their attendant idiosyncratic needs, whether they are total physical or intellectual impairments? For example, in my opinion I should be known as an academic with an individual form of Friedreich's Ataxia. Why am I being standardised?

The feeling of being standardised as a 'customer' is unfair and unprincipled because it fails to look at me as an individual and an academic, thereby undermining all my hard work. I found this to be a truly aggravating approach from management staff who only considers me to be a person with an obvious disability, as opposed to an individual who happens to have a disability. This gives rise to the stereotypical assumptions that group all people with severe disabilities living in shared-supported accommodation as 'customers'. Maybe I am only one of the few people with a severe disability who suffers from such a stereotype. Maybe it is because I am one of the few people with a severe disability who has performed hard intellectual work for a PhD, the significance and achievement of which is being reduced by my disability. Should I not feel unhappy?

The outstanding problem then is this: the service provider's failure to identify diversity in disability. Rather, all managers and staff seek to call all residents living in shared-supported accommodation under a spurious cultural and economic term – 'customer'.

Here are my personal feelings on the subject. How can such spurious name calling be of benefit to the service provider? Like every business, even not-for-profit organisations have the need to undertake cost–benefit analyses. This then becomes a method to enable the standardisation of disability supports, enforcing a one-size-fits-all policy, thereby providing service providers with an economic advantage.

I recently visited another facility under the same disability service provider as a prospective resident, or customer, if you will. Despite this fact, the treatment I received when I arrived was second rate. Nobody on their management team decided to show, or even follow up with a post-visit email. I'll be honest here: on looking at the residence, the general equipment and resources, for me, presented a situation that could possibly meet my individual needs. However, because of my disability I require some elements of individual care. For example, I need to be showered with an ongoing hygiene regime that can take two-and-a-half hours every morning. This is provided at my present residence, despite there being a working ratio of four support staff to nine residents (4:9). As part of my first visit there, I asked about their care regime and was told, rather abruptly, that the morning routine for each resident was completed within a time frame of 45 minutes. This concerns me, because they have a working ratio of 3:5, three support workers to five residents. In my well-educated opinion this is an indication that there may be a poor working ethos, where there is a failure to respect and support the individuality of humans at this facility. This is not to say that where I currently live is perfect; the care provided is still standardised to a great extent.

In the Melbourne care facility for people with disabilities where I live there have been major changes to my lifestyle in recent times, caused by a combination of overcrowding and understaffing. Consequently, we are very aware of the decrease in the ratio of disability support workers to residents that has been evident in recent times. At the moment, as I have already mentioned, there are four support staff for nine residents. It is the service provider's policy that two of these support workers must always be present in the house during the active part of the day, so they can assist with routine matters that may arise, and any transfers in and out of the residence. However, this significantly constrains the community access of residents. Let me give an example of this from one day, prior to my birthday, in June 2015. That day there were no staff to assist me in getting community access. My preference for this day usually involves food of some kind, shopping or movie watching. Even though the experience of movie watching for me is a dwindling pleasure, due to increasing blindness, going to the movies has allowed me to find some comfort in joining with others in this public enjoyment.

At that time we only had eight residents in the house. Now we have nine and one wonders whimsically if this adds to our rent increase or not?

This lack of opportunity to have and form accessible community engagement is just the starting point for why I feel socially impoverished. I am speaking here as a sociologist. Social policy somehow lets us down when we need it most, when our rubber should be hitting the road. Sorry for the joke but this is not funny.

Rising Rental Fees in Shared-Supported Accommodation

Why am I so outraged at being stigmatised by the bogus name calling of all residents who are stereotyped by the unauthentic word 'customer'? Possibly because this standardisation leads to some selfish penny-pinching tactics with some negative effects on residents, many with high-support needs, as outlined below.

At a meeting to discuss an increase in residents' rent, we were told of our provider's plans to sell off some of their prime real estate in Melbourne's central business district. A resident asked a question about the way in which the provider was viewing this sale. The ensuing discussion seemed to suggest that the sale would assist the provider in overcoming budget problems, and was the principal reason why, as a corporation, it was considering divesting itself of some assets.

The suggestion was put to the provider that if the building in Melbourne's Central Business District was being sold for budgetary purposes, a small amount of the proceeds from the sale could be used to help the pensioners among the residents overcome their budget problems that would result from the increase in the rent.

After all, the service provider is keen to present itself to the community as an effective not-for-profit company, with all of its profits ploughed back into the community it is serving. And residents certainly wish to have their part in this community recognised. They are not merely renters; they also constitute part of the provider's community.

The provider retains its assets to enable the provision of the service it is contracted to provide.

We residents living in shared-supported accommodation already pay a substantial amount of our pension, about 55 per cent, in rent. Keep in mind that the source for most of this rent money is the Australian taxpayers. I would imagine that they, the taxpayers, would prefer to support a welfare policy of social equity, and recognition that we are all equal citizens of this nation.

The Commodification of Rent and Disability Support Services

There are many pressures associated with the provision of disability support services. We all know this whether we are residents, workers or managers of support facilities, or officials of the Department of Health and Human Services (DHHS). We are all under the pump in an economic climate where there is widespread political anxiety about budget blow-outs and a possible collapse of our entire financial and economic system. We all know this. So when I make my professional contribution, as a resident of such a healthcare facility, my recommendations and pleas are complex.

I would ask that readers appreciate that I too am a citizen, a member of this polity, one who has paid my taxes, one who has worked persistently to promote the common good. Yes, what I am about to say is framed in my own interest, but it is not only that. I am just as much concerned morally as any other non-disabled professional person about the serious state of our disability support services. Unless that is understood then my point will not be appreciated.

Nevertheless, there are very important issues that, I believe, have not been and are not being, addressed and adequately communicated to residents like myself who are affected by these decisions. I am taking the risky route of admitting that I don't know all that I should, even if I am compelled by my professional responsibility to continue to speak up. Those who know me, and who find it almost impossible to follow my slurred speech when my speech-therapy trained personal carer is not in attendance will readily see the irony in my determination to 'speak up'!

When I studied sociology some years ago we confronted the fact that impoverishment begins from a lack of accessible community engagement. We pay well over half of our pension in rent, and the service provider now seems to have decided that this is not enough, and so they wish to increase it. Granted, the service provider is a not-for-profit that pays all funds it receives back into the organisation. But then with all these rising costs, why should the brunt be worn by reduced social interaction by those who most need it? Am I simply adopting an envious or greedy ideology to suggest that the management side of the operation should also have its salary and entitlement budget reduced?

The world is changing – we all know that – and stringencies are increasing all the time. But do disability service providers need to take money from pensioner-residents to pay bills that should have been anticipated, such as overcoming a deficit in rental income? Where was the forward planning when the service provider accepted the contract to house us residents?

My somewhat provocative questions are these:

- Why can they not reduce funding from other parts of their bureaucracy, for example from their well-paid management?

- Why is the rent increasing beyond most residents' affordability?

If the increase in rent is justified as being unavoidable, we might well ask what we receive in return. The issue of rent is problematic; it has a potential, if not handled justly, of giving the impression that we residents are just a commodity to keep the welfare-service show on the road. Any rent increases must be economically justified because we live in a residence that is lawfully subsidised to house people with disabilities. And most who are on the disability services pension require 24-hour support. So it is not just a monetary, commodity, thing.

Let me again be very provocative here: the major political parties tell us that their new federal–state relations have brought about new and allegedly efficient economies to social welfare and health. OK, it is from our taxes that our political parties have been paid and are running election campaigns. Large amounts go to the political parties to prevent them from going bankrupt. So where is the public education material that has explained clearly and simply how these new latter-day stringencies have come about for disability support services? Why is there such widespread anxiety among those concerned about the rejigging of costs from the federal to the state level? If there is no extra impost upon those who can least afford it, and financial obligations have merely been balanced in a new way, why has it not been explained clearly and unequivocally?

One probable answer is that the political parties have not actually been willing to engage in such positive political education. They've been too busy trying to tweak support by a politics of negation. Maybe then, public funding for elections should be cancelled until these privileged parties can demonstrate that they are able to engage in political education in a just and fair way.

Choose Equality

My continued effort to express my deep disagreement as publicly as I am able, has a great deal to do with the provider's management policies with regards to my shared-supported accommodation facility where I live with a group of people with various disabilities.

I have developed my role as an advocate of social justice over the last four decades. During this time, I have had to find ways of remaining positive despite my disability – a blight that is not of my own making. My current lifestyle includes regular efforts to raise my voice by writing feature articles. These are not just a hobby, believe me, and they are important to me in terms of how I perceive my self-worth as an active participant, and a resident with something worthwhile to say.

I cannot help but recall my efforts to support myself before I came to this shared-supported accommodation. When I moved here, I assumed I was going to be supported in my labours to maintain a degree of personal control over my own situation. Yes, my condition is a progressive one and so my abilities are not exactly the same as they were before I moved here six-and-a-half years ago. This change creates a paradoxical situation, a tension between what is and what could be? Still, I have had to live with this tension for 41 years. It's not just something that has popped up for me as an issue with this service provider. But at times I feel as if the senior managers of my service provider have a serious case of mental paralysis!

I am a rather sensitive fellow; I will admit that. And those who hear what I have to say should try to keep in mind that I have had to learn to read the responses of people who find it difficult to relate to me, and I suspect, to other people with disabilities as well. I concede that not everyone has the talent of empathy, of instinctively developing a 'synergy' with guys like me. So forgive me for saying this: over the last six-and-a-half years I have become dismayed with what I sense is the response of the service provider's top management. The message that comes through to me, and I believe to others as well, is that they are adopting a manner that treats us (me included) like fools. I believe that there's a serious 'disconnect' here.

The resulting impression is that management lacks integrity. They do not seem to understand that their approach sends disabled residents ambiguous messages. It comes across as if the service provider's major problem is all about retaining top management in the lifestyle to which they have become accustomed.

I know what I am saying here is blunt and if I still had a voice you would have heard me shouting. Believe me, I am trying to stay sane and say these things with an element of humour even though this exercise has made me upset. Frankly, I'm worried about the impact of these changes to budgets and payments upon my ongoing contribution. While big changes are being made at federal and state levels, residents should not be expected to take a significant hit to our lifestyle nor should we be expected to hide our worries and concerns.

The division between the roles of the state government and the federal government, for example, is causing much confusion. A crucial question here is will the rental allowance still be a deductible item in a federal system, when it's a state-run organisation? That is just one question and I'm sure there are more.

I can understand that the service provider has real budget issues. But it is still we residents who provide (yes, provide) the organisation with its purpose. Without us the organisation wouldn't exist. That needs to be kept in mind when budget policy is implemented. There needs to be a genuine expression of equity across the entire organisation and residents should not be made to feel they are the organisation's cash-cow.

Genuine equity should be a known preference for the service provider's top managers. Let me be frank and specific. Is it possible, in the current climate, for the disability service provider's top management to become genuine public advocates for an ethos of equality across the entire organisation? I would have thought that they are corporately bound to uphold and safeguard the much-needed equitable and pragmatic functions of service providers (support workers) and residents in shared-supported accommodation. But how can they actually do this without becoming political advocates of a fundamental change to how senior management is configured legally, and to how their high wages are calculated? This seems to me to be an important nub of the problem. Are senior management in some way legally prevented from speaking out against the unjust inequities that accrue to themselves as senior management?

Increase the Rents and This Will Be the Result

To extend this line of argument, let me draw attention to the possible consequences for disability pensioners with any increase to their residential rents. One thing is for certain, it will mean a corresponding reduction in disposable income and an increased potential to become trapped in poverty.

Consider, our pension is a fixed living allowance; that is, it is carefully calculated to allow people with severe disabilities to live a life where some form of amelioration becomes a real possibility. We also must not forget the prevalent reality that most disability service providers carry the banner and highlight the fact that they are charitable not-for-profit organisations. 'Choose equality!' is one service provider's logo. It's emblazoned on everything it publishes. Just who are being chosen for 'equality' here?

But how does the choice of equality fit with service providers who are known for their core involvement in care for people with disabilities, when comparatively very large payments go to top-level managers? What is their remuneration package? How does it compare with average weekly earnings? It is not exactly a salary bordering on destitution. So then, why are Australia's most vulnerable people put at further risk, by allowing people with severe disabilities to absorb the budgetary restraints? 'Choose equality', indeed!

Somehow our understanding of political responsibility needs a fundamental rejigging. We need to redefine 'advocacy' so that it is not put under the constraint of corporate capitalist values. Those who are corporately responsible to implement equity across their welfare organisations, like senior managers, should not feel that they are prevented, by some or other subtlety in corporate law, from publicly advocating just economic and income distribution. To do so should also mean promoting salary cuts for those at the 'top end of town'. Let them show that they 'choose equality'!

If we want to build a just economy, with an equitable system of welfare provision, then we should encourage social welfare providers, and they should also join in the effort, to develop such a self-denying approach to management!

'Choose equality!' Let us move away from slogans and 'smiley face' manipulation to genuine welfare, and to genuine equity.

Some Thoughts from a Friend on My Situation

The following is from my dear friend Bruce Wearne back in 2015, in an article he co-wrote with me:

> Peter should not have to plead his own case like this. He is not hanging out to be treated as a 'special case'. He is simply appealing for support workers, who take the time to understand him, who are willing to learn from him how they can learn what he is trying to communicate. He is not saying this is easy; he knows that all too well. It is not just about what disability support workers can learn from him about his condition and how to be supportive, their friendship extends in all kinds of ways just like any friendship does. Moreover, he is concerned about their situation, and in particular, their work conditions.
>
> And so Peter is particularly concerned about a form of management that assumes that he is simply a somewhat passive recipient about what is provided to him by the service provider. He's keen to emphasise that he is wanting to see the

emergence of a facility ‘ethos’ in which residents are respected for their active responsibility. Being a resident does not mean passivity when it comes to promoting justice and fairness for all.

Chapter 8

People with Disabilities and the Concept of Synergy

"I have characterized the social struggle as centrifugal and social solidarity as centripetal. Either alone is productive of evil consequences. Struggle is essentially destructive of the social order, while communism removes individual initiative. The one leads to disorder, the other to degeneracy. What is not seen – the truth that has no expounders – is that the wholesome, constructive movement consists in the properly ordered combination and interaction of both these principles. This is social synergy, which is a form of cosmic synergy, the universal constructive principle of nature."

- Lester F. Ward (Wikipedia)

Here are a few articles of mine written on the topic of synergy and support workers. These articles are rewritten to follow the purpose of this book. I reflect my thoughts on the importance of synergy, and the vitality of the working relationship between a person with severe disabilities and their support worker.

It should also be noted that this experience was different for me from when I was living alone and first wrote on synergy, to where I am currently living now in shared-supported accommodation.

My progressive illness creates a deterioration of motor skills, leaving all my physical attributes severely disabled. However, I am still able to perform research and write pieces like this book. Basically, my performance is made possible through the power of synergy gained mainly through my work with my support worker and a long-term academic associate.

Let me explain why I am taking the opportunity of emphasising this concept of synergy in this book. For me there is a synergy with various people who help me to get my views across, which is crucial for me and I dare to say for the disability sector, let alone for people with such different abilities and their support workers.

My complaint is simple; it is also a fear. This tendency of casualisation in the workforce undermines the ethos of the place where I live. I find myself alarmed by the reduction in the friendships I have been able to form with my support workers. Casualisation frightens me because it requires constraints upon the synergies I need to keep going, at a time in my life when my energy is reduced. Perhaps further discussion can pinpoint ways in which casualisation changes the ethos of our living place, our homes.

This tendency is confirmed when the need to nurture genuine lasting friendships between residents and support workers is misunderstood. The unpriceable nature of friendship is not that it is worthy without worth; but its worth actually transcends the fair dollar value of the service.

And that misunderstanding at the level of the managers working in supported shared accommodation hollows out the ethos of service delivery because it lacks the attributes necessary for sustained caring of the residents. But there is an 'altruistic' outcome in the social service delivery of which I am the beneficiary. It happens in the workplace, which is also 'my place', the location of such synergy. It generates friendship – workers and residents become 'mates'. This workplace is where we actively prosper through such synergistic outcomes, and where we welcome the visitors into our home. 'My place' is sustained by the friendships that are generated there.

In other words, I am suggesting that the relationship between a support worker and a resident is what this is all about. This is also an industrial issue. We cannot deny the relationship factor involved in caring for people with disabilities. The management of facilities that are providing the services must come to acknowledge this if people with disabilities are to gain their full potential and respect in society. Just policies are needed to ensure that carers will stay around as an important part of our life! And it seems, sadly, that such an insight is foreign to the political horizon of our major parties and the governments they form.

Am I suggesting that the organisation running the facility where I live should become more political? Yes, I am. But I am suggesting that they need to do that by emphasising policies that will embody justice and fairness. That is the way service providers can make a positive contribution not just to the lives of its residents and its workers, but to our wider society and our responsibility for each other as fellow humans.

Altruism, Passion, Empathy, and Pragmatism

I want to discuss altruism, passion, empathy and pragmatism as four key factors in forming and maintaining mutually beneficial partnerships in social service delivery, for those members of our community who are dependent to a large degree upon the work of support workers and of other kinds of support.

The protocols of the service provider where I live in shared-supported accommodation, suffer from a poor ethos. I am quite sure that they were not expecting me in this house, and I too never expected to be in this situation. But even though we have to make the most of this unfortunate state of affairs, it is not going to prevent me from saying what needs to be said.

The service provider has a real problem. Rather than having a set of policies that emphasise procedures formed individually with the needs of the cared-for person front and centre, they seem to be stuck with operating in a standardised way. Such standardised procedures simply do not provide people with severe disabilities with adequate support. Even if their standardised approach qualifies as being 'best practice' under some managerial criteria, we are simply too complex for their modus operandi.

My complaint also has to do with the ethos of the place I live in.

Let me begin with what I experience all too often. My friendships with my support workers are unfairly reduced in a variety of ways by the managerialist presumptions of this service provider.

The faces of our support workers are the first that we see in the morning and the last we see at night. I am keen to preserve the basic friendships that are keeping me going, even as I find my body simply slowing down.

Moreover, I do not want to personally identify any individual manager – although there are some I have come across who come to mind that possibly should be exposed, but I will restrain myself. My aim in writing this is to promote some sustained soul searching among those managing the service provision. I'm writing this against a background of service delivery that is simply not good enough.

Lacking are the key attributes necessary for caring for people with severe disabilities. These missing attributes are what I wish to identify in this book. They are, as in the title of this article, altruism, passion, empathy and pragmatism. These, I believe, are what should characterise the caring service provision for people with severe disabilities.

There is no doubt, that passion and empathy are required if social services are to do the work they claim to be doing. One needs to develop empathy in order to overcome one's instinctive aversion when faced with social problems by instead facing the people involved. And passion is what gives the necessary drive to a person delivering some or other social service. It is fundamental to enabling human life to flourish.

Altruism

With respect to altruism, I am reminded of a famous quote from Adam Smith (1723–1790), an important founder of modern economics. Smith wrote and published The Theory of Moral Sentiments, and later, wrote The Wealth of Nations. He refers to self-interest, but it is important to note that he is actually focused on how the morality of the common good is promoted when a job is performed with self-interested passion, leading not only to the advantage of the worker but also to those served. In this sense, altruism is better understood as the effects of self-interest, not selfishness.

> It is not from the benevolence of the butcher, the brewer, or the baker, that we expect our dinner, but from their regard to their own interest … We address ourselves. Not to their humanity but to their self-love, and never talk to them of our own necessities but of their advantages.

I sense that something like this principle is working itself out in my relationship with my own support workers. As it is commonly understood, altruism is about selflessness, it is a principle or practice of concern for the welfare of society. My situation seems to be endorsed by Smith in the above quote. In the social service delivery of which I am a recipient, and which involves a personal-care attendant, the 'altruistic effects' actually work themselves out in a workplace that becomes a friendship circle where workers and clients are mates. This workplace is actually our home in which the residents are actively welcoming the visitors. It is not only those paid for their work who have an interest, a general self-interest, in forming what takes place. After all it is also a place sustained by the friendships that are generated.

Passion

Passion is defined as a strong or extravagant fondness, enthusiasm, or desire for anything. In my opinion the ability to love what you do well has a positive flow-on effect.

Empathy

Empathy is the psychological identification with, or vicarious experiencing of, the feelings, thoughts, or attitudes of another. To have empathy concerning people with disabilities is the possible key to the social inclusiveness for many people with severe disabilities; this must be based on the pragmatic education of equitable logic. Empathy is the ability to understand and immerse in another person's perspective. For example, what we believe or think may not be the same as what really is.

So then, why is empathy so poorly understood, and frequently misinterpreted?

Pragmatism

Sometimes the practical way to get good things done requires some elaborate theory and research. Sometimes you can forget all that and rely on present knowledge and common sense. Do whatever works to achieve what you, or the people you're working for, think is worth achieving. That's an obvious principle for practical reformers. I think it also applies in an important way to academic thought and research. Some of the most fruitful research can be intellectually unambitious.

Altruism, Passion, and Empathy in Pragmatic Synergy

To be passionate in disability service provision must mean a strong desire to assist, to make better and to maintain what would otherwise not be available. Empathy is to show that you have the ability to put yourself in the other person's situation.

Pragmatism is to defy academic theory and use common sense to believe in what makes sense. These are terms that should be more broadly used at all levels of the disability sector. We are all humans in the disability sector. We require individual forms of care, for whatever is needed with the money government provides. But then not-for-profit disability service providers can squander such funds by using a large portion of these funds to pay a relatively small number of managers and administrators. And, in that context, we have to ask whether the management is adequately appreciative of the altruistic effects of the disability workplace, and of the passion, empathy and pragmatism that are the necessary components of a vibrant social delivery in the places where people live.

I am suggesting that the relationship between a support worker and a resident in shared-supported accommodation, is what this is all about. We cannot deny the relationship factor involved in caring for people with severe disabilities. Management of disability service providers must acknowledge this if people with severe disabilities are to gain their full potential and respect in society.

Of course, service providers should be fully passionate and empathetic about the friendships that can be fostered between people with severe disabilities and support workers. There is need for what I would call pragmatic reflection here and the emergence of a general approach in which the personal care of support workers is infused with new synergies from relationships with the people with severe disabilities they serve.

This is about sharing passion and empathy. It will involve a pragmatic orientation to work towards mutually benefitting outcomes and the formulation of common goals.

Considering the relationship between attendant carers

and the people they care for in terms of a dynamic mutually beneficial partnership means that people with disabilities are assumed to have many different abilities, many of which are waiting to be disclosed. This line of thinking may well help service providers encourage a more inclusive society.

I wonder why, with all my academic knowledge and deteriorating disability, my thoughts are not considered more, and taken to be worthwhile and useful by those in the management of service providers.

My considered suggestion is that the ethos needs changing with a renewed and sustained emphasis on altruism, passion, empathy, and pragmatism.

Partnership Benefits for People with Disabilities and Their Carers

Can mutually beneficial partnerships be the key to a better future?

Let me explain why I believe mutually beneficial partnerships between people with disabilities and support workers can play a fundamental role in highlighting the many different abilities that people with severe disabilities have, and how this nurtures positive life chances for them.

For some time I have been pondering the question of whether the disability workforce can find guidance from what I have referred to in some of my writings as the 'synergistic' outcomes that result from the interaction of people with disabilities and their support workers. I am convinced that in many instances this is also needed by management, to help them make their contribution in the disability sector.

Consider the dynamics of mutually beneficial partnerships between those employed to nurture and those being nurtured in the disability sector. In this relationship, these people, rather than being merely disabled, often emerge as those with many different abilities: abilities that can reciprocally assist the carers in the other (sometimes non-work) responsibilities that they also have. Just one example of this is that I have been able to help my carers find suitable books and articles for their studies, but there are many more.

To explore this relationship fully leads us to consider some pragmatic examples of how these people who are being cared for are actually contributing in all manner of ways to a more inclusive society. In my case, the synergistic partnership I experience with my support workers allows me to flourish in my role as a disability activist. And I'll presume to leave my support workers to speak up and nail the positive contributions (sometimes I guess not so positive, too) that I make to their (non-working) lives.

For example, the synergy that is provided to me through the intervention of flexible disability support provides me with the means to achieve many of my goals in life. This approach to personal care is cohesive, flexible and humane. It allows me to manage the complexities of my life and desires. It helps me to attain my full human potential when and where my bodily abilities are lacking. For example, my performance is created by the synergy gained mainly through the work of my support workers.

Synergy for people with different abilities and support workers is about life chances and the creation of opportunities. Therefore, the essence of synergy is to actively value difference; and difference is a must for many people with different abilities.

The Effectiveness of Synergistic Relationships

In this context, synergy for the disability workforce is a way to provide the correct form of guidance for people with different abilities and support workers. To have an inside-out approach is about life chances and the creation of opportunities. Therefore, by initiating an inside-out approach we confront the support workers who sometimes sees him or herself as a person languishing at the lowest, grass-roots level, and who consequently needs the disability sector for employment. We need to turn this around. In my view, a synergistic approach to the disability sector is not just about better help for the disabled person – it is about raising the status of all involved and ascribing due respect.

Effective Working Relationships

These effective working relationships should be given the respect that is due for their rightful contribution to models of leadership. Why are these highly successful working relationships so often below the radar when it comes to forming social welfare policies for the disabled?

Could it be that these highly efficient working relationships are simply out of sight and out of mind? Is that why they seem to attract such a lowly status when it comes to the common ideas that are assumed to be relevant when it comes to making improvements in the disability workforce? Maybe we need to look again at the manuals that are written for workers and develop a distinctively new theory of management. Why not?

The synergistic approach I advocate might be best seen as an inside-out approach to the management and organisation of the disability workforce. It will demonstrate public confidence in the abilities of the people who are served to exercise control over their own lives.

Let me try and explain this 'synergistic' model of workplace leadership in more detail. In order to make sure that this kind of model is flexible enough to allow change, even if complete change does not take place, the aim is to avoid an approach which sees the disabled person as a problem and instead reckon with such a person as a 'problem-solver', just like anyone else, and just like the support worker as well. In this, a synergistic model develops a distinctive understanding of societal inclusion.

The Flow-on to Management of Service Providers

The promotion of resident involvement in all matters of staff selection and recruitment needs to be considered from a pragmatic standpoint, rather than merely remaining satisfied with policies that are captive to a remote theoretical overview. And if we can indeed overcome this problem the flow-on will be to all those in society who are indirectly and directly related to disability.

A Synergistic Approach to Disability

Here is my proposal for a dictionary definition of synergy:

The interaction or cooperation of two or more organisations, substances, or other agents to produce a combined effect greater than the sum of their separate effects; for example, the synergy between artist and record company; or between disability support workers and people with disabilities who have high-support needs.

In some of my writings I have referred to what I call the 'synergistic' outcomes that result from the interaction of people with disabilities and their support workers. These effective working relationships should be given the respect that is their due since they make an indispensable contribution to ongoing efforts to devise effective models of leadership in such workplaces.

It may be highly contentious to say outright that disabled people are second-rate citizens, but if so much of our social value is measured by income then maybe 'second-rate citizen' is exactly what that income disparity tells us.

In the Disability Field, Does Love Conquer All?

The best form of care is, of course, supplied by family members or close friends. These are those whose support is supplied by love. They are living testimony that love conquers all. Love is mighty and powerful, particularly when administered with compassion, empathy and patience.

I have come, much to my own surprise, to another related conundrum: how can the medical model be modified to avoid a standardised approach to disability care that simply confirms mythic stereotypes about seriously disabled people? I struggle daily with the way the facility where I live in shared-supported accommodation is managed. I am therefore wondering whether at a deep, cultural level its modus operandi presupposes the medical model. I'm wondering: is the organisation somehow stuck in a rut assuming that we residents are actually 'sick', and that our lives are basically structured by illness?

I'm not saying that all the residents are free of physiological problems that require special care. I am not even thinking here primarily about physiology; I am thinking about the way in which our 'roles' are understood by the prevailing management. Are we, in effect, occupying the role bundle of the person who is sick, who is subject to medical care?

Over the course of living on my own for 21 years I had two long stays in hospital, but all in all my educational conquests have far outweighed any medical complications. This has me thinking: I'm living as part of a situation in which I have been confronted by nothing less than the reality of what I have referred to above as 'the social model'. This is a situation that will be endorsed by most people who have physical disabilities without any intellectual impairment.

This reflection about synergy, love and the management of the disability sector, leads me to encourage us all, particularly public policy researchers, senior management in not-for-profit organisations and elsewhere, to think carefully about the 'who?' question when dealing with the severely disabled people they are committed to serving. This certainly means that an ethos of equity is needed along with the legislated provision of further assistance. It will require political courage to ensure that an ethical culture is developed in which people with disabilities who have high-support needs are cared for individually and effectively.

My desire to rise above the privations of this shared-supported accommodation fuels my motivation for this and also many of my previous written works.

Friendship and Service Provision Ethos for People with Disabilities

I want to discuss an aspect of the standardised procedures set by service providers in facilities that serve disabilities. More to the point, I am keen to explore how this affects the ethos of service delivery for people with severe or profound physical disabilities within such shared-supported accommodation.

Let me be utterly frank. The ethos of service delivery in the house where I live has lacked key attributes that are necessary for caring for people with disabilities. Admittedly, I have sought to draw attention to this deficit by a constant effort to raise awareness. An organisation's ethos takes time to change. Nevertheless, the jury is still out with respect to whether we are experiencing a positive change. I am concerned that the friendships I have made with support staff be respected by a form of management that recognises the benefits that occur because of the personal synergies that arise from the work done.

There is a simple need to be able to enjoy life as an individual, in a way that is the same as the individual aspects of dignity that are part and parcel of the much proclaimed 'freedom of choice'. I want to ask: has the 'right to choose' become a ploy of many service providers? The principle is conveniently displayed in marketing and other public relations material. But is it about staying on the politically correct side of government and public opinion? After all, it can be argued by many living in shared-supported accommodation that the self-interest of top management has been placed well beyond the reach of the people with severe disabilities whom these facilities are established to serve. Our support workers don't just perform abstract functions; they are people just like the people they are employed to serve.

This state of affairs is why I am taking the opportunity to write this book. Our friendships with support workers need to be defended.

In part, this place of residence fails to administer an

appropriate assessment of my specialist medical and social needs, one of which is human companionship. This place needs to function in ways that allow the residents with disabilities to solve their own individual problems even if the house is managed under the protocols of a service provider. And the workers should be respected as our friends.

Chapter 9

The Interview:
Social Space with Economic Room to Move

"Looking at worldwide trends, the pattern in countries with supposedly the most progressive records of inclusion is that the most severely disabled get left behind, i.e. an even smaller minority even more segregated."

- Jenny Cooper

I am an advocate for the seriously disabled. For those who know me, that may not come as much of a surprise. They know the condition that has affected me like a pain in the backside for decades. But as my condition has progressed so has my eagerness to become an activist. But first, a word of explanation.

The following interview was initially sparked by my dissatisfaction with my own situation. This dissatisfaction is not new to me, and in fact for a long time I have become accustomed to giving voice to my dissatisfaction. Nowadays, though, I find it more difficult than ever to communicate, which consequently increases my dissatisfaction. My typing used to be at the rate of two words a minute, but this is no longer possible. I asked my friend Bruce Wearne to assist me, and, knowing my situation and my concerns, he suggested this interview.

By tossing around these issues together, we can explore the social context in depth, and identify some aspects of caring for the disabled that are too easily overlooked. Then, with his help in editing what I have already previously published, I can put forward my views in a way that will not only emphasise the needs of severely disabled people like myself for 'space with room to move', but I can also take on the role of 'disability consultant' and offer advice to those who have to confront and resolve complex managerial issues that cannot be avoided when care is given. I know about these issues because I have studied them, first back when I started a business studies course at Dandenong TAFE (Technical and Further Education) in 1985. I did this course when I came down to earth with a bang. I could no longer live in a fantasy world and I needed to create my own future for myself.

I don't want sympathy. I like to think that one of my skills, which I share with many others, is dodging the sympathy people instinctively have for people with a disability, and instead I seek to promote empathy among members of our society. The creation of a just society requires the recognition of all members of society and their many and varied relationships, including direct and indirect involvement with political processes.

So here is my interview:

Bruce: Peter, let's begin by talking about space and movement. These are basic aspects of everyone's life. But since you were 14 your body has suffered a condition that changes your view and constricts your experience of space and movement. Can you tell us a little about how this has happened?

Peter: As mentioned earlier [in this book], I have had to

struggle with Friedreich's Ataxia since I was a teenager. I was 14 when this was diagnosed. It is a progressive disease causing impairment to the nerves and a failure of timely muscle reactions throughout my body. The messages sent from the brain via neurotransmitters are slower and weaker than they should be.

Bruce: And so, muscular growth is hampered, giving rise to various bodily problems.

Peter: Problems, but let's not have any fantasy about this – these are severe deformities that I've had to learn to live with. It's a condition that increases my limitations as I live longer. For example, I have had to deal with severe scoliosis and cardiomyopathy. By 23, I was reliant upon a wheelchair, but now I'm simply too uncoordinated to make use of an electric one.

Bruce: So that means you need help in just moving: an activity that people usually take for granted.

Peter: That's right. But remember what I said about 'empathy' instead of 'sympathy'.

Bruce: Let's come back to everyday movement issues

after we explore this important distinction you make. Can you give me an example of where 'sympathy' is like a kick in the guts?

Peter: Yes. I completed my PhD in 2006, and I tried to gain employment within the not-for-profit disability sector. I applied for some positions that I was very well-qualified to fill. Take for example one position where the pay was very minimal for 20 hours per week at $20 per hour. Even within the sector the response was very unsatisfying.

Bruce: Are you just complaining that you didn't get the job?

Peter: Well, yes and no. You confront a mindset. There's always lots of sympathy. But to employ someone with my qualifications, even in the disability sector, requires a structure that is empathetic. Budgeting needs to think about employment that would require a personal assistant even for a basic position. So, it is structural, but it is very personal when you have to deal with being told your application is not successful.

Bruce: And then you are saying that sympathetic structures are such that your condition gives selection committees an opportunity to trim the list.

Peter: Exactly. Sometime after another failed application I learnt the following: 'Having interviewed Peter for a temporary job, his disabilities made it difficult to employ him despite his insights and contacts' (Media Player, 2008). That was a response to one of my On Line Opinion articles regarding employment in the disability sector.

Bruce: So you're sure that the person who wrote that was full of 'sympathy'. But making you a hero for not getting the job doesn't get you very far does it?

Peter: Exactly. It has been 20 years' hard work, in that case for not much at all: just another humiliating comment that lacks empathy.

Bruce: You mean that by putting it online in response to what you wrote it actually does the opposite of what the person intended to say?

Peter: I guess so.

Bruce: OK. Let's take this distinction between sympathy

and empathy that is so basic to your push for justice.

Peter: Fine. Fire away.

Bruce: Well let's discuss getting out of bed, or getting into bed for that matter. As your condition has progressed, this means that you have needed more and more assistance. We won't go into all the messy details although I get it can easily get messy for you.

Peter: Sure. Yes, let's keep to say the sociological and economic aspects of what's needed.

Bruce: How do you mean, Peter. Is getting out of bed and going to the toilet a matter of sociological and economic significance?

Peter: Of course. You taught me that. What happens to people like me with staff shortages? Or say there's some staff problem. Do I have to wait for six hours between shifts to urinate? Or think of what might happen in terms of rashes between my legs if somehow things get out of hand? If my skin gets infected I am in a lot of trouble.

Bruce: So you're saying that if places like where you

are living now are registered as institutions that care for people like yourself, they have to be able to do so.

Peter: That's it. Because my condition has progressed I have had to learn patience and truly I am a pretty patient person. I do try to stay positive. I can't exactly throw a tantrum. But I have lived with this for a fairly long time already, for over 41 years, in fact.

Bruce: Now you're a PhD and you've obviously been so expertly trained in sociology (Ho! Ho!) to closely observe the things that go on around you. I've also been trained in this way! And what you say about the need for a structural dimension to empathy is very important, I think. But in recent months I've observed that your emails have had an edge to them that I hadn't ever noticed before. I mean one of the things I have always noticed about you is your happy-go-lucky demeanour. Now as your condition progresses I guess it's natural to get frustrated. But, tell us a bit about these recent frustrations. I think the people who are reading this might benefit if you do so. It might stimulate a better understanding of the empathy that is needed.

Peter: Here's not the place to go into all the details of rights and wrongs. I'll give a few examples of problems I have noticed that irritate me.

Bruce: Go ahead.

Peter: Take for instance my current academic support worker, Christina. She does a lot of work for me. But such support is not mechanical like a cog that can be replaced. She's a person. My typing speed is a real pain in the arse. I cannot do what I want to do; I have to rely very much on Christina to do the typing. Now this has also shown me the importance and potential of 'synergy' developing between people. Now you can say that all she does is my typing, but if she was to be replaced I would lose that relationship, that's synergy.

Think about my support workers. There are constant changes with regards to my support workers. Why is this? It seems to me that 'He or she is only a support worker!' is a stereotype just as bad as 'Oh, he or she is disabled!' Such shallow thinking actually destroys the potential of developing synergy. It also means that empathy won't get a look in. To put this in economic terms:

the 'personal aspects' are reduced to 'disutilities' and therefore can be disposed of.

Bruce: So, by continuing to write you are actually trying to show 'empathy' for management and those who work with you, even if, as you repeatedly have pointed out in your articles that they have to work under the very dehumanising restrictions imposed by neoliberalism!

Peter: I'm just as selfish and self-oriented as the next person. I just really try hard not to take any notice of actions that are based on stereotypes.

Bruce: But you have. You are. You've been really irritated.

Peter: I guess so. But as my disability gets worse, I find it harder to avoid the stereotypes. I am very much aware of how negative, and emotionally and socially destructive they can be. So, I will still always be trying my hardest to combat stereotypes. And as I said, I am also aiming to improve social awareness through my writing.

Bruce: So, Peter, here you are in a 24/7 care facility – with all of its strengths and weaknesses – and some of the problems you've been facing, how do you, as a resident, think you are being treated here as a highly qualified 'disability consultant' from Melbourne University?

Peter: Good question. Let me refer to issues of safety for example. Some of these I've addressed earlier [in Chapter 3, in the section 'Dignity of risk should be a disability right']. But there are other sides to this.

Bruce: You've mentioned to me the contentious issue of your sling. You used your former sling for a long time.

Peter: Yes, let's take my sling as an example. I used that old sling when I was being lifted in and out of bed, and in and out of the bath, and in all kinds of [other] lifting for 15 years – 15 years! But then when I came here this was not acceptable to the service provider. I was told its service provider's policy on these slings had changed because another person with a disability had died as a result of using the sling.

Bruce: Yes, the technology in that sling was clearly insufficient.

Peter: Of course. And if it was shown to me that it was dangerous in the same kind of way then I'd have to have a new sling. But what I'm wanting to say is that I am very sensitive to being standardised – the sling is just an example. I guess it is also a matter of feeling in charge of my own life.

Bruce: So, you're saying that's the issue here; that the changes to your life when you move out of independent living to a new facility with on-site supportive assistance need to be fully negotiated. And I guess you'll say that that also needs 'empathy' and a willingness to ignore stereotypes.

Peter: It's a matter of respect and being respected. With our concern for safety – I'm not denying the need for taking due care – we need to be careful we don't standardise people with disabilities.

Bruce: Or standardise managers as 'merely bureaucrats' who standardise people by rules?

Peter: I guess so. But I can't go home at night. People who live with the kinds of disability my body makes for me want to be looked at and respected on an individual basis.

Bruce: So you are taking the role here of advocate for disability, not just criticising out of self-interest?

Peter: I hope so. For instance. As I have thought about my worries I remember that I felt really hurt that they wouldn't even let the sling I had used for 15 years be tried out, so they could see how it worked. Now that was insensitive. After all, the day before moving in here I had been using the sling. And to refuse to see how it worked seemed to me to be saying that my life up until then somehow didn't count, at least not in terms of their management of my disability. Well that's wrong. They should not assume I am going to reinvent myself by coming to a new place.

Bruce: So this is Dr Peter Gibilisco, Disability Consultant, giving advice then?

Peter: Yes, and I'm not ashamed to take that role even if it is on a pro bono basis. I spent many years studying sociology and economics. I'm not completely unaware of management theory.

Bruce: That was an important part of your reflection on stereotyping wasn't it?

Peter: That is right. Think about it this way. It was not just the sling. As you've said, I'm usually a pretty optimistic fellow. You have to be if you are going to tackle life with this condition. You're up against what I call the medical model.

Bruce: You better explain that.

Peter: People with disabilities are first, presumed and believed to be medically inferior, which then becomes society's systematic norm – they are simply a cost – and that leads to cumulative disadvantage. It involved a complete rearrangement of the technology and equipment I have been using and which has helped keep me going for many years. Then, all of a sudden, the equipment that I was using did not meet the organisational safety standards for people with disability. As I suggested. It's as if something in the standardisation process wants me to forget just how much I coped before I came here and how. And to put it in pure materialistic terms: such a move to standardise disability has cost me a lot of money and created a bit of emotional turmoil.

Bruce: So, you are somewhat surprised by what you have encountered. I guess you have known all about it from your studies of sociology and economics. The kinds of hands-on lack of empathy can get under your skin. So let's try to look at what needs to be considered for a person like yourself, who has to make the transition from relatively independent living – with outside support coming to your house – to supported living which needs to develop structured 'empathy' to enhance a resident's genuine independence when most day-to-day household affairs are taken care of.

Peter: I was first told about the house when I first applied for an increase in my Disability Service Register [DSR]. This house presented as a possible alternative to an increase in the DSR. This seemed a good option to me at the time, since requirements for a DSR were strict and the facility promises comprehensive care and oversight.

Bruce: So you could also say that as your condition

progressed there were other constraints like pension and health benefits that were tightened and made the move somewhat more attractive?

Peter: Yes, I've been trained to see the flow-on effects of changes to regulations. People in my situation need others to remind them of these changes to the legal requirements.

Bruce: What do you mean by comprehensive care and oversight?

Peter: I'm referring to disability service provision. It has to do with the way a facility must present itself to the community it serves.

Bruce: Yes, I recall reading your critique of the State Disability Plan. You've said that it is full of rhetoric that gives a good impression, but in actual day-to-day delivery there are hurdles. Are we dealing with something similar here?

Peter: Yes, I think so. I have thought a lot about this. Don't get me wrong. The plan has an impact on independent living and also upon supported living. There are things that worry me. How do I make my voice heard without being misunderstood?

Bruce: It's not easy communicating and making your needs known when your muscles don't let you talk as clearly as you would like.

Peter: Exactly. I will have difficulties communicating with anyone let alone the management. How will they reckon with the fact that I am a PhD? I'm not a person with a cognitive disability and it would be unfair to stereotype me as one.

Bruce: So you feel in a bit of a bind, then? Your speech is now very slurred.

Peter: Sadly, yes. And when you want to stand up for yourself you don't want to give the impression that everything is wrong.

Bruce: Keep going. You've done a lot of thinking about this.

Peter: I'm pretty clear why I'm not happy. I feel as if I haven't been listened to.

Bruce: As you say your condition makes it hard for you to put into words why you are unhappy.

Peter: Exactly. That's why this interview format is helpful. I've had to think a lot about why I am worried and to check myself that I am not just over-reacting. But I'm not. I know I'm rather selfish at times. And yes, there's a management issue about dealing with people with my qualifications who want to speak up, let alone with my condition. And when you are running a place like where I am there has to be some kind of standards. But my problem is that I feel as if I am stereotyped.

Bruce: There's a wide range of people to be cared for. I guess there's not too many PhDs who are being cared for in these kinds of facilities. I guess there will also be those with cognitive and learning problems.

Peter: Exactly. And it's not that I'm wanting empathy only shown to me. I've got to show it too, I guess. You've got to have standards and safety, and things like that. But I've been used to living on my own for 21 years and using the sling for 15 of those years. And I had to manage my own life in different ways from what is now required. There were things I found worked for me when I was living in my own place, before I came here. And I know that my condition is progressive, so that the basic methods of lifting me and what I can and can't do will change.

Bruce: So, this interview you've got me to have with you is to explain that you feel like you've been standardised. A bit like a MacBurger. We touched on that in sociology: McDonaldisation it was called. Standardisation in hamburgers. And you are saying it feels like that at times here.

Peter: Yes. Exactly. Management these days seems to have a similar standardised approach towards all types of disability. I can appreciate that a place needs standards, but one of the standards must also be to listen or, in my case, take time to listen to what it is I am trying to say. Yes, it's difficult. And I wasn't the easiest person to communicate with even before my speech was slurred. But if I said to the management that I felt as if I had been stereotyped in a negative way they might think I was just criticising because I was feeling sorry for myself.

Bruce: And are you?

Peter: What?

Bruce: Feeling sorry for yourself?

Peter: To some extent, yes, I guess. But I want to point out that my disability is very different from that of others who live here. And I'm not just concerned about me. The sling issue has a flow-on effect to others, like support workers. So it is not just my personal needs here. I know that.

Bruce: One last thing. In one of your earlier articles you discuss mobility and your friendship with Rob of Frankston Radio Cabs, your maxi-taxi driver. You are obviously concerned that those involved with caring for the disabled give due recognition to the need for people to move around. The concept of mobility needs to be opened up doesn't it?

Peter: When disability is viewed in terms of the medical model, 'mobility' is understood in a very restrictive way. I'm wanting a shift towards a more feasible social model. How could I ever say that a person is no good, unless they are physically mobile? But if the medical model prevails that is what tends to happen at the expense of what I would call the perspective from a social model of mobility.

Bruce: Sociology has its own understanding of social mobility. And I guess the availability of computers, let alone wheelchairs, keeps you going, helps you to keep on pushing. I hope this interview also does that.

Peter: The coffee machine is over there; just help yourself to a cappuccino!

Chapter 10

Where is the Dignity in 'My Future, My Choice?'

"We continue to stay in denial of who we are and still succeed as a nation. Disability is a part of who we are. Inclusion would acknowledge that destiny may one day lead us there. Or there's always revolution!"

- Jenny Cooper

My disease was progressing severely, but nothing could equip me for the extreme loss of control of my life I was about to face in a shared-supported accommodation facility. Sure, because of my very slurred speech I have difficulties communicating with management, but they should reckon with me as someone who is qualified (I do have a PhD and have studied sociology, economics and management). And if they are not taking my opinions into consideration, then they should know they are making me feel as if I am a person with a cognitive disability. I am very supportive and sympathetic of many residents in this house who have cognitive disabilities, but I am not one.

I am also supportive and sympathetic of the workers. They need to be encouraged to take the views of clients – in this case people like myself – into account. One of the major reasons prompting me to decide to move to this new place had to do with my personal well-being. It was no longer safe for me to live on my own. This was basically due to the fact that the Department of Human Services (DHS) had held back my Disability Service Register DSR. Throughout my years of requiring adequate support, I've never had my pleas for additional support totally accepted. I argued consistently and logically with DHS for an increase in my DSR over a period of two years, with my disease progressing all the while, partly exacerbated by the emotional turmoil created through insufficient care.

Basically, DHS gave me $69,000 to cover all my care costs. At the time, I wanted to increase this by about

$30,000, which would allow me further care in addition to that provided in the morning and evening service, thereby alleviating some of my vulnerability.

Although I have done a lot with my life, DHS were opposed to my request for an increase in DSR even though, at least in terms of the rhetoric, 'mutual obligation' is the current political buzzword.

One of my major problems was the situation I faced in having to deal with casual staff. During the last two years of living on my own in Dandenong, I was in charge and managed the employment of caregivers in a direct way. One day, my main support worker was unwell. At short notice I needed to come up with an adequate replacement. I'd heard good reports about a service provider, however, I found that the support worker whom they provided me with was inadequate, mainly due to their inability to understand my speech. Recently, where I am now living, casuals from this same service provider have reappeared on my horizon.

One thing that prompted my move to shared-supported accommodation was my need for 24-hour care. I was being left on my own, and thus highly vulnerable, in between the regular times of care. One day, for example, I fell to the side of my wheelchair. The same thing happened on another occasion as I will explain below. But because of the restrictions on my support I was consequently alone, and left in an alarming position.

Just consider: one day, at around 8 pm the staff came to my room to deliver mail; they found me lying half out of my chair and partly on the floor. I had fallen into that position an hour earlier. Unable to reach the buzzer, I was left while vomiting and yelling for one hour. I had just finished dinner.

In other words: I know very well what care I need. I am all too aware of the vulnerability of my situation.

Then, on a Friday night I received confirmation that my new DSR was approved. This proved to be a lifesaver in so many ways. I just hoped that my new DSR level would ensure a better level of safety for me.

But sadly, the move to shared-supported accommodation that occurred did not necessarily mean I was better cared for.

Recently, in the middle of the night, I was in a very uncomfortable sleeping position in bed, so I called for assistance by using my buzzer. No one turned up. I heard the next morning that those on duty could not find my room key to come and assist me. Then, later that day, my father came to visit. Straightaway he looked at me and asked if I was OK, because he could see I was not. Of course, I asked him the same question back, because it was strange of him to turn up suddenly. It transpired that he had received a call from staff, at 2 am, informing him of the situation, and mentioning that they would call him back if they couldn't access my room. But since then he'd received no further calls. Understandably, he was worried and decided to visit me.

This episode was irresponsible, especially when they had already contacted him, a 75-year-old, at 2 am! And, anyway, it begs the question: why had the casual staff not been properly informed about the location of the keys?

I'm sorry to report incidents that have caused me immense pain, with physiological and psychological suffering that is unbearable and borders on torture.

Of course, it is easier for those providing services to standardise disability. The manager must remain in control, although standardising the way in which services are delivered causes serious difficulties for those who are cared for, and also for carers. A person's real-life situation needs to be taken into account.

Having a disability does not necessarily mean that you are mentally impaired. Service providers of not-for-profit services seem to want to standardise disability to make it more amenable to organisational processes, which can then distribute work tasks according to an economically oriented calculus.

Let me provide another example of another incident when, once more, I fell out of my wheelchair, on Tuesday, 19 March 2013.

It was just after dinner. I needed to empty my bladder, and as usual, my carers set me up in the appropriate way. But in so doing I slumped out of my chair, falling to its side. After waiting five minutes for the staff member to return, I decided to try to make myself a little more comfortable by moving a bit. But that movement had the opposite effect – my body involuntarily flung me forward and... crack. My hip was broken.

The staff member arrived 30 seconds after this happened. I was in great pain and finally managed to convey to them that they should ring for an ambulance to take me to the hospital.

I repeatedly requested that I be taken to a private hospital as I had private medical insurance coverage. But due to my slurred speech and being in a lot of pain they had very little chance of understanding what I was trying to say.

The ambulance transported me to the Dandenong Hospital where I was duly X-rayed and my broken hip discovered. They gave me pain relief leaving me feeling much more comfortable for an operation the next morning.

The operation was successful. However, I had a major problem with the drugs that were administered. I was put on an eight-hourly regime of two tablets of Valium and one of Endone. I have a history of hallucinating with such a high dosage. My issue, at this point, is that no one thought it important to tell me the dosage of these medicines.

My hallucinations were very severe – I imagined terrorist attacks and believed my life was under threat. Before you laugh at me, please try to put yourself in such a situation. It sounds ridiculous but it was extremely difficult for me to get over the emotional turmoil that was created by these terrifying hallucinations.

My real need, now, is to exit this place where I have no control over my own life. The people making decisions for me are repeatedly making standardised decisions that leave out the most important factor – my true needs. This has been a recurrent aspect of the last few months that I've lived here, and the troubles I have had to confront.

It has become so difficult for me to express myself and to get my needs identified. Writing as I am doing now is my only way of communicating these issues. Due to my disability, I am not in a position to freely communicate, even on paper. If the support worker is not used to my speech then they have to wait as I reply to their question with my typing speed that sometimes can't go faster than one word a minute. This is why I require the 24-hour care of a primary carer. If incidents similar to those I have recounted here recur, the carer would be aware of my preferences and of my medical history and know my needs. For example, they would direct me to a private hospital since they would know about my private medical insurance coverage, and they would also be able to oversee the medication given to me.

As I said, I know what I am talking about. Things have got to change. A new attitude is needed to face the reality of caring for those with severe disabilities. I hope this straight-from-the-shoulder piece can help those who should be thinking about these matters.

Chapter 11

The Standardisation of Services for People with Disabilities

"Convictions are more dangerous enemies of truth than lies."

- Friedrich Nietzsche

Efficiency Verses Effectiveness

The State Disability Plan is not the only endorsement of the need to emphasise individual care for people with disabilities. We now hear of a profound new development – person-centred planning – which is said to be the worldwide benchmarked best practice. This involves a highly individualised vision of the person with disabilities, resulting in care needs that multiply into a kaleidoscopic variety of individually generated special needs and concerns.

This attempt to generate a sensitive and compassionate approach nevertheless faces an ongoing dilemma. The costs associated with such an approach to the provision of disability services continue to outstrip the services that can be provided by the pension. Moreover, the demands (and possibly the false needs as well) that are generated by this latest example of neoliberal micro-reform of the 'disability workplace' have the effect of further transforming the already precarious environment for care-workers and the residents.

Let me change the topic slightly here and note how in these days of cut-throat public relations, the provider may be confusing the services it provides with its own slogans. Let me invent a possible slogan:

> ACE DISABILITY SERVICES – We are here to give independent and fulfilling lives to people with physical, intellectual and multiple disabilities.

Lovely slogan isn't it? But then reflect upon the efficiencies that are required in shared-supported accommodation like my own. And now look carefully at that phrase: 'people with physical, intellectual and multiple disabilities'. I am not criticising the ethical intention; I am trying to draw attention to the organisational chaos that will result for workers and residents if a facility conflates physical and intellectual disabilities. And who can tell how care for those with 'multiple disabilities' can emerge in the midst of such organisational blurring.

There are many residents, perhaps an overwhelming majority of up to 80 per cent, in supported accommodation with some form of intellectual disability. Therefore, it can be expected that in shared-supported accommodation, such as where I reside, for many service providers where there is a policy of taking on high-demand people the result will be the standardisation of disability care. Don't get me wrong, the intellectually disabled are also my neighbours and they deserve proper care. But by putting all people with all types of disability together in one facility, even if there are different classifications on paper in a provider's policy documents, there will be an inevitable drive towards standardised care and abstract efficiency. This may allow the provider to continue its 'service provision' but it will be at the expense of the individualised care.

Quite seriously this is what I fear will happen. Without appreciating that residents are genuine members of the community that the service provider is maintaining, a policy will develop in favour of standardisation over the appropriately differentiated individual care needed for people with severe disabilities in shared-supported accommodation.

Disability service providers are given substantial sums to provide for the care of people with disabilities. These payments come from a variety of funding sources, including from government payments, and donations from both not-for-profit and for-profit companies, as well as from the public. Among residents of such facilities in the disability sector there is a suspicion, deeply ingrained, that these funds never seem to meet the needs for which they were intended. Requiring service provision to be subject to a competitive tendering process means that service providers, which were once considered to be not-for-profit organisations, are now driven to accumulate the trappings associated with business success. This includes providing CEOs and senior management with excessive salary packages, while they remain cut off from the day-to-day reality of the people who use their services.

Like everyone else, people with disabilities are highly individual. This individuality makes life complex. When people with disabilities are recognised for their individuality and diverse needs, the individual treatment they require becomes apparent. That is the moment when due respect is needed.

Yes, branding costs money, which is fine if the benefit resulting from new logos is spent in not-for-profit service management rather than in more remuneration for the top management. It is the responsibility of any company's management to ensure it has a positive public image, and this isn't achieved by merely selling off assets to wipe out a deficit. After all, a black-ink entry on the bottom line of a company's account books is a useful tactic to divert attention away from any organisational dysfunction, including any moral bankruptcy.

Disability Support Services – Effectiveness and Efficiency

I'll be frank. There are many difficulties to be faced when providing disability support services. We all know this, whether we are recipients of in-home care, one-on-one support, residents of shared-supported accommodation, workers, the management of disability support services, or even officials of the DHHS or NDIS. We are all under the pump in an economic climate where there is widespread political anxiety about budget blow-outs and a possible collapse of our financial and economic system. We all know this. So when I make my professional contribution, as a resident of such a healthcare facility, my recommendations and pleas are complex.

Many of the problems in disability support services arise because it seems that efficiency demands certain generalised procedures, such as a person working in a well-organised and competent way. When dealing with disability support, effectiveness is also a crucial characteristic that needs to be balanced against efficiency. Something's 'effectiveness' is the degree to which it is successful in producing a desired result.

There have been developments at the level of federal and state government funding – negotiated through the Council of Australian Governments (COAG) – that have brought about significant changes to the delivery of human services generally, and disability support services, in particular. I do not have access to a research facility in order to adequately assess and evaluate these changes, and although I regularly seek advice from those who may know, I do not want readers to presume that I have mastered the details of all the complex agreements, contracts and policies that are now in place.

In all this, within the political sphere dominated by neoliberalism, comes the mechanism that can negatively impact on social decisions, which is the seemingly over-riding criteria: what is this efficient and effective procedure doing to enhance individual profit?

Some social decisions, concerned with human-related social services are, and should be, unrelated to efficiency.

But there are also some gross inefficiencies, I believe, that are part of the disability support sector that have little, if anything, to do with disability support and everything to do with supporting and benefitting the organisational and managerial structure that claims to be supportive of disabled people. The management of service providers are required by their own charters to produce a positive result in their financial returns. There are some unscrupulous service providers in the not-for-profit disability sector. In recent times I have complained to the management of my own service provider about their failure to disclose provision money in their accounts. Provision money is meant to be part of rent money, which is our money conveniently used by staff to pay for our groceries or food for the house. Under no circumstances does this money belong to the service provider or its staff members. Such not-for-profit enterprises will follow the model of service provision that I would call the neoliberal streamline model. In simple terms, it interprets organisational and managerial reality in a way that instinctively requires financial profit to have precedence over people's welfare.

I do wonder why a not-for-profit organisation needs to show a profit. I live in a shared-supported accommodation residence, supposedly in the not-for-profit disability sector. Are we, the residents, simply to roll over and allow ineffective and abstract efficiencies to prevail? Do we really want a neoliberal perspective, where efficiencies mean money saved, while effectiveness means costs, which are therefore a challenge to the sector's viability?

This state of affairs prods me to drive home an ethical perspective about residents in shared-supported accommodation. In this house we have nine individuals with high-support needs. In other words, what is required for residents in shared-supported accommodation are processes and resources that overcome a lack of human support. There are a lot of funds paid, however, more is required for the unmet needs of disability support. This is my considered conclusion, which I have developed during my many years of living in the face of a progressive disability.

The disability sector has lost its way by being caught up in the self-interest of an overloaded pool of management, and is in danger of creating a greater need for more financial assistance!

But all is not doom and gloom. There is a plausible and workable solution for many of the current failures in the disability support sector – direct employment techniques, which, through the possible resulting cost savings, will actually empower people with disabilities. Direct employment techniques have been used to positive effect by DHHS and presently under self-managed funding by the NDIS.

In 2009, when the direct employment scheme was formally introduced into my home state of Victoria, Australia, I was involved in the initial pilot programme. This is a key reform for disability services, which offers numerous benefits and is something that many individual support package (ISP) users should consider. Direct employment is a person-centred approach to disability, allowing people with a disability to contribute to the community, and so enhance their community inclusion.

In July 2013, I was keynote speaker at the Disabilities Support Professionals Conference at the University of

Sydney. There I spoke with my computer voice about Kate (pseudonym) a 46-year-old lady with a severe intellectual disability. She is involved with direct employment, with her self-planning carried out by family members. As a result Kate now lives a more inclusive life. She is supported by three workers whose rosters, pay, training and other work conditions are managed by her family, with her sister-in-law and brother managing the accounts and finances. Kate, and her mother, take responsibility for the recruitment, training and day-to-day management of Kate's workers. Thanks to direct employment, Kate is receiving the support she needs, she is happier, and she is living as an individual in the community in the way she chooses to live. Kate's family are the professionals involved in her support.

When encouraging such forms of disability support with a focus upon social coherence, it is important to ensure the arrangement is flexible enough to allow some changes from day-to-day, even if a complete change does not take place immediately. The aim is to re-build trust and flexibility in disability supports, thereby creating both community inter-dependence and independence.

Direct employment offers flexibility, allowing people with disabilities to choose the support staff they prefer, helping them to lead their own lives and allowing them to make their own decisions. Direct employment caters for an individual's support needs and lifestyle, which is after all an important concern for people with disabilities. It allows for a more personalised approach rather than the efficiency driven approach taken by not-for-profit organisations that are constrained by having to make a profit. As a person-centred approach, I believe direct employment is an important reform picked up by the NDIS as self-managed funding; this will be the key to the future lives of many disabled people and their families!

Let's hope so.

Another Torturous Episode

Are all humans told they must live their lives in the same way? No, they aren't. What, then, about those humans with severe physical disabilities who are unable to control their own lives with limited dignity of purpose and determination? And what about the different abilities of those in group homes, such as mine, whose care cannot be standardised, but for some ridiculous reason – usually neoliberal – is. This gives me a sense of not being in control, the effect of which is to make me feel punished.

Here is a recent example of something that happened to me. I was sick with the flu and, in addition, my care and support – required to keep me safe from physical injury and harm – was proving to be inadequate. One evening, I slipped out of my wheelchair three times, leaving me in great pain. Unfortunately, the way I had slipped made it impossible for me to press the buzzer to alert staff. Eventually, I was discovered by a support worker, who popped in to see me on a random visit. I was left in great pain, exacerbated by having to deal with the flu at the same time.

The next night, I was left with three support workers who couldn't understand a word I was saying. This meant that I had to wait until 8:30 pm for a support worker to arrive who was capable of understanding me; instead I gave up, had dinner and went straight to bed.

But it got worse. The next afternoon, I slipped out of my wheelchair once again. Of course, by this stage I was feeling very tired. Being in an uncomfortable position, I decided that the only way for me to feel relaxed was to pull myself up by the sides of the table to make the wheelchair fall, thereby putting me in a more relaxed position. Again, I had to do this by myself. When I fell, my feet pulled the buzzer cord, which alerted the staff.

These events have had an extraordinary effect on my heart, which is something I had to have further check-ups for in the following weeks. Hence, that weekend became a manifestation of my loss of control and my feelings of being punished. This incident is one of the many examples illustrating the lack of dignity and choice I have living in a group home.

To Emphasise the Inadequacies of a Loss of Control

I am assuming that I am just like everyone else in that when I have a 'situation' it is primarily up to me to deal with it. But then there are aspects of my 'situation' that most other people don't have and never will have, so they don't have to deal with it. There is only so much a person can put up with before it wears them down.

Here I am, then, in supported accommodation for the disabled.

The support staff I presently have cannot offer me the support that I need to adequately confront my situation because they are not part of a one-on-one support system. They may help me live life in a way, but their help does not sufficiently address what I can't avoid, which is my 'situation'. I still hope to make a contribution as I struggle to live each day with Friedreich's Ataxia; I have the intellectual ability to do so, but this is lost on many people, even if this ignorance is based on negative stereotypes that have no basis in reality.

Success for me, like for many others, is an ongoing dream, but I tell myself that I must be realistic. I have had to learn the discipline, the painful discipline, of living within the confining frustrations of Friedreich's Ataxia and its associated problems, including the social ones.

Please hear me out. I simply want to live my life as

much as I can on my own terms; that is, I'm happy, and even eager to play the best hand with the cards I've been dealt. This is my first priority. If this seems like a cry, it is not a cry for sympathy, but instead for empathy. Please, please think about that.

Now here's the 'thing'. Within disability support, individual integrity needs to be respected. Moreover, an individual's integrity cannot be avoided. That being the case, if efforts are made to standardise an individual's care then such standardised support seems to be provided for self-interested reasons. It is sad to say that this is how the modus operandi of service providers like my current disability service provider are perceived, not just by me but also by some of the workers who have to work within their constraints.

When I initially entered my present group home I was as upfront as I could be when outlining the deterioration of my body under this form of Friedreich's Ataxia. That reality hasn't gone away for me, but it doesn't seem to have registered with my service provider. Today, I am now in a situation where my Friedreich's Ataxia has progressed further, while I am expected to live, function, and continuously make my contributions under the inappropriate protocols and inadequate, impersonalised care. All the while, my personal interests seem to be ignored. In short, the management policies that govern day-to-day life here fail to provide disability care that respects and enhances individual integrity.

Let me go one step further. With regards to my greatest need: in a day-to-day sense I am wanting to assist those charged with caring for me to understand my failing ability to communicate, mainly via speech. My being able to engage in conversation on a practical level is of immeasurable benefit and importance in slowing the progression of Friedreich's Ataxia. Consequently, I am convinced that one-on-one support, facilitated by self-managed funding, is the most appropriate form of care for me at this advanced stage of my declining capacity. This, I believe, is basic to meeting my individual care needs even at a minimal level.

My support workers in this care facility do not have enough time nor do they have the understanding of my particular stage in the progression of my condition to assist me properly. This is not to criticise them, since they also have eight other residents with very different and varied disabilities to care for as well as me. The support workers from my current disability service provider don't even have the time to try and satisfy all my needs, most of which are related to my 'self-definition' as a professional and are therefore related to my academic pursuits.

Let's put it logically with this brief definition: a support worker for a person with high-support needs must have the time, patience and empathy to support them, individually.

I have noticed – I have been unable not to notice – that time is a major factor with my current disability service provider's modus operandi because their form of shared-supported accommodation restricts care for me in my 'situation'. We have four support workers and nine residents residing in this house at any given time. With the current working ratio of support staff to residents, even a good measure of individualised care becomes an impossibility.

OK, then, let me spell out how I see my needs: I need

at least two hours a day for a one-on-one conversation with a support worker. And the support workers here do not have the time or the ability to (learn how to) understand me. My speech is hard even for me to understand even if I know my own intention.

Many unfortunate past incidents, such as falling out of my chair, could have been prevented with the provision of adequate and personalised care, but this provision must first start with an understanding of my disability. The problem with my falling out of my chair happened again just the other day. Similar to the previous instance, when I stooped over, I thought that the only way for me to feel relaxed was to pull myself by the sides of the table to make the wheelchair fall; this was to put me in a more relaxed position. I will not point fingers at a specific support worker, but rather it is a 'human resource deployment problem' (as they might attribute it in management textbooks) where effectiveness has been overridden by efficiency. Once again, I stooped over in a more painful manner and I was not able to help myself in any way. I was in this position for one-and-a-half hours.

I acknowledge that recently my disability service provider has tried to rectify past situations, but as yet their attempts have not made any noticeable changes.

I have tried to write positively and frankly. It seems now that it is of utmost importance that any ongoing solution will require a support worker or workers to spend more time with me in order to understand me and my disability better. This is the only way they can know what my needs are and how they are to be met. My needs can never really be identified by simply applying a cost–benefit analysis.

I am conscious that I am putting a serious challenge out there to my service provider, and to the employer of all the residents' support workers.

Chapter 12

Can Disability Stop You from Believing in Yourself?

> **"He who fights with monsters might take care lest he thereby become a monster. And if you gaze for long into an abyss, the abyss gazes also into you."**
>
> **- Friedrich Nietzsche**

A Bucket-List Trip

In telling this story about my recent 'bucket-list' trip, I may appear to come across as being angry, so I will try my best to paint it in a more light-hearted way.

A 'bucket-list' trip is one of those special trips you make during your lifetime. It is something you have always wanted to do before your days come to an end. After my recent experience of planning a special trip away, on this occasion to Thailand, I may be able to offer some advice for those planning their own, final, bucket-list trip.

Speaking pragmatically, it is important to be flexible when planning and managing such a trip. To be otherwise is neither appropriate nor practical. For example, many who know me and the circumstances of my trip question the formulaic approach taken by my disability support services provider. All of which means that I must be realistic about the mistreatment meted out to me in my present circumstances and carefully consider my future prospects regarding this kind of venture.

My recent trip had a severe emotional impact on me, but, please, I want no sympathy on that score. Instead, I want to discuss broadly the modus operandi, the facts and the figures behind the disability service provider's 'vacation policy' as it applies to those of us in shared-supported accommodation. It is claimed that this type of accommodation offers 'quality, sustainable and individually flexible services'.

Consider what follows to be a case study of my service

provider's vacation policy.

Despite all the obstacles I had to face, I was determined to give this trip a whirl. The outcomes can be hugely beneficial. A trip like this certainly doesn't have to be a disaster, and, in fact, it can be quite an adventure. Anyone who has disabilities like myself has their own individual issues to surmount, of course, so there will be some pros and some cons, but it can be enjoyable for everyone, including the carers. For me, and many others like me, the greatest burden is financing such a trip.

My trip to Thailand was something that was driven by my dreams and desires as a person with Friedreich's Ataxia. I wanted a no-holds-barred bucket-list trip, and I planned on doing this within my limited budget.

I have never been shy about pursuing my dreams, but, together, my disability and my so-called service providers have turned this already difficult task into an almost impossible one.

The Disability Service Provider's Vacation Policy

Disability service providers are supposed to deliver individual support to all residents, as opposed to the standardised style of care provided in many institutions. Although, in a general sense, we are all disabled, there is a vast difference between individual residents when we consider the complexities of biomedical matters, and the socio-economic and physiological problems concerning our disabilities. It is a fact that all disabilities are different.

So why does the disability service provider have such 'cookie-cutter', formulaic policy when it comes to residents' vacations?

I should point out that previously I had been on a trip to Hawaii with the assistance of two support workers from my service provider. At that time, I paid for all flights and accommodation, and other smaller expenses, like food, while the service provider paid for the support workers' annual leave. But the introduction of the new policy has greatly affected the extent of this financial cost for individual residents, like me.

I planned the trip to Thailand with the assistance of my regular, and very much appreciated, shared-supported accommodation support workers, as well as the work performed by my academic support worker. However, about two weeks before Christmas, I was informed of the new vacation policy's onerous rules. This policy was read out to me by a support worker who also handed me a copy.

I read it carefully with the help of my support workers, and learned that in addition to the cost of my carers' flights and accommodation I would also have to pay something called an 'individual support package', which rises every financial year, according to the Consumer Price Index (CPI); so, in January 2017 when this trip took place, this amounted to about $44 an hour, 24 hours a day.

This financial impost added about $1056 per day, per carer, to the cost of my trip. Such a cost, for a very physically disabled man like myself is an impossible hurdle. After paying rental allowance and other necessary extras to maintain my life, I am left with a disposable income from my pension of about $200 a fortnight, besides unforeseen costs. This leaves me with very little money to save.

This policy was initiated in March 2016. The whole process of organising my trip frustrated me so much that I made some stupid mistakes concerning my processes of care. In wishing not to subject myself to the service provider's vacation policy, my key carer had previously resigned from the organisation and my other carer was privately hired in Thailand.

I planned to pay for all my key support worker's travel expenses – including food and flights, an equivalent standard of accommodation to my own, and an upfront bonus of $1000, as well as a worthwhile gift. This was all the money that I had at the time. I tried to do it fairly, so I could create a win–win situation for my support worker and me.

I have two issues with the vacation policy.

First, this policy does not recognise that 45 per cent of people with disabilities live in poverty. Why is disability and poverty so hugely related?

And, second was the fact that I was unprepared for my choice of care on what was to be a momentous trip for me. I had my heart set out on taking my current and trusted support workers from my home, but because of the service provider's vacation policy, this was impossible. This was disappointing as this trip represented so much, and it was likely to be my last because of my deteriorating medical disability.

Was this the bucket-list trip that I had planned? Despite my initial anger and frustration, I could have thought more clearly and developed a correct response in these situations. In hindsight, I believe a bucket-list trip should never be hastily planned, and we have to make sure that all socio-economic plans can be fulfilled.

Chapter 13

An Explanation of Life and Some of Its Pursuits

> **"He who has a why to live can bear almost any low."**
>
> **- Friedrich Nietzsche**

Because of the severe socio-economic and medical restrictions faced by those afflicted by Friedreich's Ataxia, many of us are constantly subjected to being stereotyped as losers and we are unfairly harassed. Our abnormal features and functions as a result of our disability don't make our lives any easier. Believe me, my experience is that many people – no matter from what walk of life – believe they know best about how a person with Friedreich's Ataxia has suffered and will then apply the stereotype to tell them what they can and can't do.

Does this sound fair to you?

My Professional Diagnosis of Stereotyping in the Disability Service Sector

Disabilities are an infinitely complex social problem with no 'cookie-cutter' socio-economic and medical remedies. Which begs the question, why do people with disabilities get stereotyped? This question needs a political answer. Personally, I think it is bound up in the winner and loser mentality of post-modern capitalism or 'trumpology'.

It's my opinion that many stereotypes are employed by those who are channelling what compassion they have to give support to political extreme movements, for example, One Nation. Is this simply a function of their lack of education, or could it not be that they have simply not bothered to give the problems of those with severe disabilities much consideration?

Let's delve further.

I want to discuss some delicate matters that are central to the power of stereotyping of people with severe disabilities. The subject of my discussion will be sex, sexuality and sexual expression. Mix the terms sex and disability and one has a power glue to make any stereotype stick. Both sides of this complex relationship – sex and disability – suffer from intense stereotyping and for unethical reasons these are encapsulated in love–hate principles: you may love or hate sex; and severe disability engenders emotions that are spurred on by love–hate factors. These emotions and factors then tend to be stereotyped. Unfortunately, some, not all, view this in stereotypical ways, and hence they are created via word of mouth or the texted word of mass and social media.

Sex and severe disability present us with an important foundational dimension of our shared humanity and, therefore, must be treated respectfully and humanely. Unfortunately for me, my Friedreich's Ataxia has allowed me to still have full sexual function, which at my age only serves to increase my frustrations. (Am I challenging another stereotype here by publicly admitting my sexual frustration?) There is a policy failure on the part of my support providers, because they do not consider my personal issues and circumstances.

From when I was 28 years old until I was 49 (1990–2011), living on my own was what I needed. It allowed me to exercise my thoughts and individual rights as a person with a severe disability. Even before that time, my life was not 'normal'. But, even so, I had my heart set on doing things that I could adequately perform, such as getting an education, including my PhD. Study was difficult, but I managed to find the correct balance between human wants and needs. Likewise lovemaking is what I would call a sensible need – a legitimate want of many people with diverse severe disabilities, including Friedreich's Ataxia. Such needs and wants are dependent on an individual's motivations to find their own happiness and the freedom of choice to participate in society as an equal citizen.

To me, lovemaking (I also mean it in its widest sense as well as the physiological) is the key means of alleviating my frustrations. It is one of the few things I can still physically perform, and something that I still have control over. But control in this matter can only be furthered by mutual respect.

Do the disability service providers actually work for the people who have severe disabilities in their care, by discovering and meeting their basic care needs? I was a direct employer for DHHS and have first-hand knowledge of the way service providers rip off the system. Is the application of existing policy just another way of creating funds for self-interested disability service providers? Or are we going to see all disability service providers – whether public or private – developing a cohesive policy to cater for the social dilemmas that will arise from a political desire to give due respect to all the needs of an individual?

I do not want to denigrate those with severe intellectual disabilities in any way, or those on the autism spectrum. But I'm quite sure that if service providers were to emphasise their concern for the individual aspects of disability within their tendering bids for contracts then they would be opening up new avenues of public awareness, where the public would be confronted with the reality of disability rather than the stereotypes.

What am I getting at? It seems to me that disability service providers are able to forget about the people with severe disabilities whom they are serving during the tendering process and simply standardise people. It is much more cost effective to place everyone in a one-size-fits-all, 'cookie-cutter' stereotype. Most people with Friedreich's Ataxia are in fact extremely intelligent; however, why is it that I continue to confront my own condition in a stereotyped misrepresentation that views it as an intellectual disability? Friedreich's Ataxia is not an intellectual disability. Let's put it in plain speech: it is just some symptoms that confuse those who will instinctively reach for the stereotype in order to ensure the misapplication of disability related stereotypes to people like me.

I want to emphasise that my concerns around sex and lovemaking are not an obsession. It may seem to have taken on obsessive characteristics because of my slurred speech and my inability to explain what I'm getting at. And maybe such appalling stereotypes are justified in so far as I realise it is difficult for people to get the point. Haven't I been tempted to think of myself in such terms and haven't I had a struggle to actually say what I now realise needs to be said, delicately but firmly? But presently, without any coordination or mobility, my enjoyment in whatever I can 'perform' in lovemaking, is still enjoyment. Getting older and wiser allows me more control of powerful involuntary movements. In turn this allows me to better understand what sparks of these. In this case, lovemaking becomes an extreme pleasure. This then allows me to feel that I have given respect and not just been respected. In other words, the control of my involuntary movements to further mutual respect makes my efforts of lovemaking, when they happen, very satisfying.

I am saying that the need to be involved in furthering mutual respect is universal and some of us need special attention to have appropriate space in which to fulfil this part of our responsibility to ourselves and to others who come into our lives.

Chapter 14

Why Do I Have to Keep Repeating Myself?

"How we sound influences how we are perceived physically, intellectually and morally. For individuals with a speech disorder (e.g., slurred/ slow speech, stuttering), those biases are often intensified leading to substantial social impact beyond the speech disorder itself."

- Adam Vogel (2015)

My ongoing request is a complaint, like the persistent complaining of a broken record. It is simply that I want to point out the fact that I have no cognitive impairments, just Friedreich's Ataxia. The repetition of this is so humiliating and frustrating, like a phonograph needle jumping grooves at a party that I am hosting. I am, in fact, just like anyone else with individual needs of my own – a point missed by many.

Yes, my unintelligible voice, poor eyesight and abnormal structure all speak volumes, and are often louder than my needs! But why do people hear these disabilities, and read them wrongly? Or refer to them as a cognitive impairment and treat me as such, instead of listening to what I actually have to say? Who configured this mistranslation of my disability; where does the translation run off the record and where does the communication get lost? Why does the line from my intention go way off the path? Why is there nobody, except a small minority of support workers in shared-supported accommodation, able to acknowledge the difference between purely physical and other types of disabilities? The problem is unjustifiably associated with the cost–benefit analyses of the self-interested. Why is there no remedial action, or training to combat this problem? Or maybe my questions are simply too hard to answer.

But why is this? Why are my complaints misinterpreted or mistranslated by many in the field of disability work? How did I get trapped in this foreign language, where only a few seem to understand me?

I haven't learned this disability dialect. It has been forced upon me, and carries with it too many tenses, with too much tension for me and my uncomplicated needs.

How many times must I repeat myself?

Dare I say it again?

How many times must I repeat myself before those who should be taking notice, do?

Can there be different, respectful and user-friendly ways of helping to seek answers? Yes, but the problem does not lie with gaining answers, but the fact that the question itself is heavily misinterpreted. Some shared-supported accommodation support workers and management in disability support services often seem to forget that we, including our disabilities, are still human beings with individual needs that must be respected.

Please, I need to be acknowledged for my needs, as I am a human too.

Support work in shared-supported accommodation is so far removed from one-on-one support. One-on-one support provides a more relaxed and individually focused environment, where there are not as many time constraints placed on support workers, allowing them the time to listen to my questions and actually understand my needs. Here, I am in control of the management of my own support workers, and they are given the chance to hear beyond my disability and severe speech impediments. To put it in this way, the phonograph will more smoothly be able to play records. I was successful living on my own and having one-on-one support from 1994–2011; during this period, I was independent and in control of my own life.

However, in my perspective, the shared-supported accommodation where I have lived for the past six-and-a-half years has jammed the needle in the phonograph altogether. This is due to the failing of some crucial processes, and allowing standardised assumptions to dictate the provision of supports. I see this clearly every day where the time needed to effectively understand me and my disability is not being adequately satisfied. At the time of shift changes and staff handover, this is highlighted further by the need for casual staff to be told about my very poor speech and eyesight, and my need for an individualised form of support. Casual staff invariably act very confused about this when I try to communicate it to them.

There is a need to show people the individual diversity of disability. This problem needs a much wider focus, and to be included as a topic in part of a Certificate IV 'Studies in disability' curriculum on the much-needed diversity of disability supports. This course helps to give disability a more mainstream focus.

There are many people with disabilities, to whom this is not recognised and acted upon. I think it is time for this to change.

CONCLUSION

This book has basically focused on the six-and-a-half years that I have spent observing and living in shared-supported accommodation under the auspices of a 'big name' disability service provider, its policies and protocols. Not-for-profit companies today, in many ways, only further the greed of self-interested disability service providers, which use people with disabilities for their own ends, and in turn neglect our true needs. For example, in shared-supported accommodation they should better cater for individual abilities and help to develop these abilities further, rather than attempt to standardise residents by giving us the spurious designation 'customer'. The term 'customer' is used to standardise and stereotype residents in order to suit disability service providers' personal objectives. As I previously stated, many of the residents in shared-supported accommodation have multiple or purely intellectual disabilities, so consequently many, or even most are not concerned by the use of this term. However, others, like me, find the use of the term 'customer' to describe residents in shared-supported accommodation very problematic indeed.

In this conclusion, I summarise some of the key chapters and the points I make. For example, in chapter five, I have focused on the political economy of neoliberalism and people with disabilities – covering neoliberalism, it is important to look to its perspective ideology, such as self-interest. This is identified by Adam Smith, an academically trained moral philosopher, in his first book The Theory of Moral Sentiments. Smith uses the term 'altruism' in his next book, The Wealth of Nations, in a way that can provide the disability service sector with valuable insights into social service delivery. During an interview with me, Hugh Stretton explained his dissent from this ideological interpretation of Adam Smith, pointing out that Smith never said that the interests which prompted people's economic decisions and behaviour were all selfish. Therefore, altruism focuses on the relationships between support workers and the residents with high-support needs, which becomes an irreplaceable friendship. In the social service delivery to which I am a recipient, involving a personal-care attendant, the altruistic effects actually work themselves out in a workplace that becomes a friendship circle.

In the next part of chapter five, I focus on equal opportunity, by critiquing three major elements: meritocracy, affirmative action, and mutual obligation. I believe it is fair to say that meritocracy can carry an extremely strengthened position concerning neoliberalism and equal opportunity.

- Sympathisers of a meritocratic approach to disability policy still assume that the base-line principle should be that people get out of the system what they put into it. That is why they seek to remove any barriers to people with disabilities putting in.

- Affirmative action, however, is all about life chances; it is an approach that requires positive steps to be taken to promote and maintain equal employment opportunity for socially defined population groups – in terms of gender, disability, age, and race – whose participation rates are reduced or non-existent due to, what might be called, 'structural factors'. Legislation stipulates that active steps be taken to promote equal opportunity.

- Mutual obligation is a belief that is structured according to the understanding that you will receive only once you have performed. The development of my education has not been viewed by the wider community as a substantial contribution because of the stigmas surrounding my disability, disutility of employers, and the failure and lack of employment opportunities I have been given. Membership in a community seems to conflict with the idea that people with disabilities and with high-support needs are merely residents who should quietly accept the second-rate lifestyle expected of them.

I then go on to discuss the NDIS. Here I am, living in a group home where most residents have some form of intellectual disability. When this displacement or misplacement is combined with other contextual factors such as an overworked support staff and to a large degree an incompetent management of the service provider, you may begin to sense how I am feeling that my lack of control is now wall-to-wall chaotic.

The NDIS scheme is based on the view that control and choice about funding provided to people will be individually driven. This will mean an important shift in the power away from the government and service providers and into the hands of people with disabilities themselves and, of course, their families. And now we look to the difference between the insurance scheme and the welfare model. The NDIS looks to provide social inclusion and this is provided through an insurance scheme, which has as its goal to provide better outcomes for people with disabilities. It is able to provide for insurance instead of welfare. That is, it looks to enhance opportunities instead of looking solely and abstractly at the first-hand, more obvious needs. With such a utilitarian outlook many welfare recipients will be stereotyped.

The NDIS is structured on the insurance model. This is to ensure social programmes are met and empowerment is encouraged. This is quite different from the welfare provision model, and in opposition to its short-term needs-based structure.

In chapter six, I examined the two ways in which disability is studied. There is a medical model of disability, which looks at disability as a medical illness that either has to be medically cured at an individual level, or controlled to allow the person with a disability to become a normal functioning member of society. Then there is the social model of disability that understands disability to be the outcome of social, political and economic processes, which have an impact on the lives of people identified as disabled, as well as on the lives of people who are not identified as such. My successful completion of a PhD – and this, my third published book – is proof of the veracity of the social model of disability.

Chapter seven asks, why is our rent increasing? If the increase is justified as being unavoidable we might have to ask what we receive in return for the increase. Rent is problematic; it has the potential, if not handled justly, of giving the impression that we residents are just a commodity to keep the welfare service show on the road. It must be economically justified because it is a residence that is lawfully subsidised to house people with disabilities. And most of us who are on the disability services pension require 24-hour support. So it is not just a monetary, commodity, thing.

In chapter eight, I discuss the importance of the synergy in maintaining relationships between support workers and residents. Support workers are the first faces we see in the morning and last faces we see at night. I suspect that these kinds of presumptions are alive and well elsewhere in the delivery of social welfare and I am keen to preserve the basic friendships that are keeping me going, even as I find my body slowing down.

The ethos of service delivery in the house where I live, has lacked key attributes that are necessary for caring for people with disabilities. Admittedly, I have sought to draw attention to this deficit by a constant effort to raise awareness. An organisation's ethos takes time to change. Nevertheless, the jury is still out with respect to whether we are experiencing a positive change. I am concerned that the friendships that I have made with support staff be respected by a form of management that recognises the benefits that arise from the personal synergies that arise from the work done.

There is a need to enjoy life as an individual, in the same way that the individual aspects of dignity are part and parcel of the much proclaimed 'freedom of choice' we have been granted. I want to ask: has the 'right to choose' become a marketing gambit by many service providers? This principle is conveniently displayed in marketing and other public relations material. But is it all a matter of staying on the politically correct side of the government and public opinion? After all, it can be argued by many of us who live in shared supportive accommodation that the self-interest of top management has been placed well beyond the reach of the people with severe disabilities that these facilities are established to serve.

In chapter nine is an interview copied from my last book, which I believe to be relevant for this book.

In chapters ten and eleven, I revisit the importance of treating people with disabilities individually. In particular, I discuss how standardising can lead to a loss of dignity and control, when there is carelessness in the provision of care.

In chapter twelve, I discuss the importance of furthering the need for social inclusion for people with severe disabilities; in doing so, I focused on my trip to Thailand, and the many challenges that were brought up in the planning process. It was to be a memorable, bucket-list trip – one of those special trips you make during your lifetime, something you have always wanted to do before your days come to an end.

In chapter thirteen, I discuss the delicate matters of

sex, sexuality, and stereotyping of severe disabilities. Both sides of this complex relationship – sex and disability – suffer from intense stereotyping and for unethical reasons encapsulated in love–hate principles: you may love or hate sex; and severe disability engenders emotions that are spurred on by love–hate factors. These emotions and factors then tend to be stereotyped.

I am saying that the need to be involved in furthering mutual respect is universal and some of us need special attention to have appropriate space in which to fulfil this part of our responsibility to ourselves and to others who come into our lives.

Chapter fourteen highlights the extent of my loss of control in this shared supportive facility. The repetition that I have no cognitive impairments, just purely Friedreich's Ataxia, is so humiliating and frustrating, like a phonograph needle jumping grooves at a party that I am hosting. Why is my complaint being misinterpreted or mistranslated by many in the field of disability work? How did I get trapped in a foreign language, where only a few seem to understand me? I haven't learned this disability dialect. It has been forced upon me, and carries with it too many tenses, with too much tension for me and my uncomplicated needs.

But disability service providers standardise diversity for selfish reasons.

Finally, this book urges readers to try and think critically about the lives of people with severe disabilities with high-support needs living in group homes. What are the drivers behind disability support, and it's these failures that promote the lack of socio-economic opportunities in life.

"That which does not kill us makes us stronger."

- Friedrich Nietzsche

Works Consulted

Cooper, J (2006), 'Inclusion our destiny?' Education for tomorrow, 88, http://www.educationfortomorrow.org.uk/2006/88inclusion.html.

Gibilisco, P (2003), 'A Pragmatic Social Democrat: An Interview with Hugh Stretton', Journal of Australian Political Economy, Volume 1, Number 51, pp, 132-142.

Gibilisco, P, (2014), 'The Politics of Disability: A Need for a Just Society Inclusive of People with Disability', CCB Publishing, British Columbia, Canada.

Gibilisco, P, & Vogel, A, (2013), 'A patient's journey: Friedreich Ataxia', The British Medical Journal, 3rd December, https://www.bmj.com/content/347/bmj.f7062

Smith, A. (1976(1776)) edited by Cannan E., An Inquiry into the Nature and Causes of: The Wealth of Nations, Cannan's Edition Originally Published in 1904 by Methuen & Co Ltd, University of Chicago Press, Chicago.

Stretton, H. (1986) 'Foreword', Public Power and Public Administration – by Wilenski., Hale and Iremonger, Sydney, pp. 7-9.

Stretton, H. (1987) Political Essays, Georgian House, Melbourne.

Stretton, H. (1999) Economics a New Introduction, UNSW Press, Sydney.

Vogel, A, (2016), 'Speech disorder is an invisible form of disability', Design for all, January, pp., 31-38, http://www.designforall.in/newsletterjan2016.pdf

Wikiquote, (2018), 'Friedrich Nietzsche', 16th October, https://en.wikiquote.org/wiki/Friedrich_Nietzsche

Wikiquote, (2018), 'Synergy', 5th January, https://en.wikiquote.org/wiki/Synergy

Glossary

Affirmative action: action to promote equal opportunities through anti-discrimination policies. They use the term quota to replace affirmative action; it is a form of positive discrimination. For example, it ensures that individuals from marginalized groups have employment opportunities.

Altruism: Actions that promote the promotions of good amongst others despite the possibility of personal dissatisfaction.

Amelioration: The act of making something better; Cambridge dictionary.

Benchmark: A standard of quality that is used to systematically acknowledge best practice.

Benchmarking best practice is a practice that highlights quality amongst given products and systems.

Cardiomyopathy is noted in Friedreich's Ataxia, which usually creates severe muscle deformities, that eventually causes the inability to pump blood.

Centrifugal: Moving away from the centre.

Centripetal: Moving towards the centre.

Degeneracy: Losing the physical, mental and moral qualities needed to sustain a meritorious life.

Diddy-squat: Anything.

Dignity: Having the right to command worthiness and respect.

Dunghill: This word can be used to describe a situation that is degraded or foul. In the Bible, a dunghill is a place where you face up to degradation. Job, in his great suffering, went and sat on a dunghill.

Dysarthria: This is noted in Friedreich's Ataxia as a speech disorder, and over time this makes communication extremely difficult.

Empathy is the ability to share the feelings, individual practices and lifestyles of others.

Equal opportunity: The right to be treated without discrimination, especially on the grounds of one's sex, race, or age.

Ethos: This is noted to be a form of business culture.

Expounded: To explain a theory in detail.

Meritocracy: The choice of people according to merit, that is, believed to identify with equal opportunity. However, this causes social immobility.

Modus operandi: Doing something in a particular way.

Raison d'être: A reason for life.

Semblance: Resembling or being similar to something.

Spurious: A term that may have a fake or disputed definition.

Symbiosis: A Greek word that defines a close relationship.

Synergy: This may be noted when two people produce an outcome greater than the sum of the parts.

Utilitarianism: The idea that a deed is good if they are of benefit to the majority.

About the Author

Friedreich's Ataxia does not affect my intelligence, but many working in the disability sector act as if they do not believe this. But the reality can be highlighted by my academic qualifications, which are a double degree from Monash University, Master of Arts from Monash University and a Doctor of Philosophy from University of Melbourne. My PhD was achieved late into the progression of my disease, when I was 43 years old. Many say to me that this was a huge achievement, and I am aware of some taken-for-granted misunderstandings about Friedreich's Ataxia. At the time of my diagnosis when I was 14, medical specialists told my parents that 'I would not live much beyond the age of thirty'. One can only imagine their response if they were then told I would obtain a PhD! These days, I still perform research and Melbourne University gives me honorary fellow status. I have written and published over 100 articles and currently have now authored three books.

However, there are many degrading effects to be battled with, such as blindness, very poor speech, hearing impairment, poor heart and limited mobility and coordination. But in all spheres of life, I've always tried my best; the jury is out, but there is still some chance that my writings may create positive change.

This book has been achieved with the assistance of two very good friends, Bruce Wearne and Christina Irugalbandara.

www.ingramcontent.com/pod-product-compliance
Lightning Source LLC
Chambersburg PA
CBHW062220270326
41930CB00009B/1798

* 9 7 8 1 7 7 1 4 3 3 7 6 1 *